Lernkrimi English History

A Lord's Revenge

Campbell Jefferys

Compact Verlag

Bisher sind in dieser Reihe erschienen:
- Compact Lernkrimi English History:
  Grundwortschatz, Aufbauwortschatz, Grammatik, Konversation

In der Reihe Lernkrimi sind erschienen:
- Compact Lernkrimi Englisch, Französisch, Italienisch, Spanisch:
  Grundwortschatz, Aufbauwortschatz, Grammatik, Konversation
- Compact Lernkrimi Englisch GB/US: Grammatik, Konversation
- Compact Lernkrimi Business English: Wortschatz, Konversation
- Compact Lernkrimi Deutsch: Grundwortschatz, Grammatik

In der Reihe Schüler-Lernkrimi sind erschienen:
- Compact Schüler-Lernkrimi Englisch, Französisch, Spanisch, Latein
- Compact Schüler-Lernkrimi Deutsch: Grammatik, Aufsatz
- Compact Schüler-Lernkrimi Mathematik

In der Reihe Lernthriller sind erschienen:
- Compact Lernthriller Englisch:
  Grundwortschatz, Aufbauwortschatz, Grammatik, Konversation

In der Reihe Lernstory Mystery sind erschienen:
- Compact Lernstory Mystery Englisch:
  Grundwortschatz, Aufbauwortschatz

In der Reihe Hörbuch Lernkrimi sind erschienen:
- Compact Hörbuch Lernkrimi Englisch:
  Geübte Anfänger, Fortgeschrittene

Weitere Titel sind in Vorbereitung.

Chefredaktion: Dr. Angela Sendlinger
Redaktion: Helga Aichele
Fachredaktion: Valerie Gulotta
Produktion: Wolfram Friedrich
Titelillustration: Karl Knospe
Typographischer Entwurf: Maria Seidel
Umschlaggestaltung: Carsten Abelbeck

ISBN-13: 978-3-8174-7663-3
ISBN-10: 3-8174-7663-9
7276631

Besuchen Sie uns im Internet: www.compactverlag.de

Vorwort

Mit dem neuen, spannenden Compact Lernkrimi History können Sie Ihre Englischkenntnisse auf schnelle und einfache Weise vertiefen, auffrischen und überprüfen.
Fesselnde Ereignisse zu England vergangener Zeiten machen das Sprachtraining zu einem aufregenden und abwechslungsreichen Erlebnis.
Der Krimi wird auf jeder Seite durch vielfältige und kurzweilige Übungen ergänzt, die das Lernen unterhaltsam und spannend machen.
Prüfen Sie Ihr Englisch in Lückentexten, Zuordnungs- und Übersetzungsaufgaben, in Buchstabenspielen und Kreuzworträtseln!
Ob im Bus oder in der Bahn, im Wartezimmer, zu Hause oder in der Mittagspause – das Sprachtraining im handlichen Format bietet die ideale Trainingsmöglichkeit für zwischendurch.
Schreiben Sie die Lösungen einfach ins Buch!
Die richtigen Antworten sind in einem eigenen Lösungsteil zusammengefasst.

Und nun kann die Spannung beginnen ...

Viel Spaß und Erfolg!

Die Ereignisse und die handelnden Personen in diesem Buch sind frei erfunden. Etwaige Ähnlichkeiten mit tatsächlichen Ereignissen und historischen oder lebenden Personen wären rein zufällig und unbeabsichtigt.

Inhalt

Story

England, 16. Jahrhundert: Der junge Adelige Edward Fortisman wird ermordet im Burggraben aufgefunden. Sein Vater Lord Fortisman schwört, den Tod seines Sohnes zu rächen. Er glaubt, Edward sei das jüngste Opfer der Familienfehde mit den Stouthams geworden. Doch war Lord Stoutham wirklich der Mörder? War er der schwarz gekleidete Reiter, der am Morgen von Edwards Tod in der Nähe der Burg gesehen wurde?
Oder steht der Mord vielmehr im Zusammenhang mit der englischen Erbfolge? Denn sollte die kinderlose Königin Elizabeth sterben, hätten die Fortismans gute Chancen auf den Thron ...
Der geheimnisvolle Alchemist Concocto scheint zu wissen, wer der Täter ist. Doch wird es auch Lord Fortisman gelingen, Licht ins Dunkel zu bringen? Kann er den Mord an seinem Sohn rächen?

Chapter 1: The Sorcerer's Cave

It was dark inside the cave and the man moved in slowly and carefully. He knew this place only from the description from the innkeeper back in the village and now that he was here, he could not stop his fear from making his heart beat faster.

"Come in," a voice said from inside. "There is no danger."

The man took his sword in his hands and walked further into the cave, the smoke thinning the deeper he went in.

"You have no need for weapons, good fellow," the voice said. "Mere weapons are useless in here anyway."

The man frowned and kept his long sword in his right hand. He wasn't sure what to expect and thought the sword gave him a certain power and security. In the soft light of the cave he saw an old man bent over a large cauldron which smoked on the fire.

"What is it you require?"

"Are you Concocto?" the man asked gripping his sword tighter, surprised to see the old man had only one eye; the other was covered by a patch. "I was told there was a powerful sorcerer living in a cave near the forest."

"I am Concocto, but I am by no means powerful. The potions I make and sell hold the power, not me."

"I need a potion that will bring a man to the end of his days."

Concocto looked up and took in his visitor. The man wore a long black coat and hid his face under a broad hat. He was surprised to see that the coat and hat were dated, of a style more suited to the time of Henry VIII and not of Queen Elizabeth. Under the hat, he could see the man's mouth and the grey beard that surrounded it.

"I have many such potions," the sorcerer said, moving from his cauldron to a shelf full of bottles and jars. "Would you like your victim to die quietly and quickly or slowly and painfully?"

Übung 1: Übersetzen Sie die folgenden Sätze ins Englische!

1. Der mächtige Zauberer lebt in einer Höhle.

____

2. Der Mann nahm sein Schwert in seine rechte Hand.

____

3. Ein Auge wurde von einer Augenklappe bedeckt.

____

4. Der Mantel und der Hut des Mannes waren aus der Mode.

____

5. Der Rauch kam aus einem großen Kessel.

____

"It's important he dies quietly," the man responded.
The sorcerer looked through his collection of potions. He picked up some bottles and held them close to his one eye to read the labels. He decided on a small green bottle and handed it to the man in black.
"Then it's important that he dies quickly," the sorcerer said. "The amount you give will decide the time it takes for the man to die."
"I need two," the man in black replied looking closely at the first bottle.
The sorcerer handed his customer a second bottle and wondered who the potions were for; it was clear the man had evil intentions. Concocto had never seen the man before.
"But such a powerful potion comes with a price," Concocto said.
The man in black reached under his long coat and counted out

the gold coins from his money bag. He was sure to pay the right amount and not a coin more.

The sorcerer frowned at the money; he normally had wealthier customers who paid more than they should. He guessed the man in black must be of a lower level of nobility or perhaps just a well-off merchant. He was also disappointed that the man had taken him so literally; Concocto had hoped to start a conversation regarding the price one pays for killing a man, the damage it does to his soul and the break it makes with his religion.

"Thank you, sorcerer," the man in black said, his voice cold and hard. "I shall return if I require more."

"Of course," Concocto replied, slightly concerned that the man had more killing on his mind. "I'm always at your service."

Under the hat, the man's mouth formed itself into a snarl, showing his yellowish teeth. He fell back into the smoke and left the cave.

Concocto went back to his cauldron.

"The evil that is inside man knows no limits," he said softly.

Übung 2: Übersetzen Sie und enträtseln Sie das Lösungswort!

ÜBUNG 2 !

1. Menge amount
2. Rauch smoke
3. Flasche bottles
4. klein small
5. Stimme voice
6. Mund mouth
7. Mantel coat
8. Geld money

Lösung: NOBLEMAN

Chapter 2: The Body in the Moat

The outline of the castle became visible as the first light of dawn broke through the low clouds. Its moat was covered by a thin layer of ice. The man in black sat on his horse behind a tree about 50 metres from the moat and, with his sword, used this early light to send a signal to the window at the top of the tower.
A woman appeared at the window, just a shadowy outline. She held a large candlestick and lit the candle. It illuminated her pretty face only briefly for she blew the candle out just as quickly as she had lit it.
The man in black smiled in the darkness, showing his teeth, and patted his horse, but he went completely still when he heard someone whistling a bright tune. Through the trees he saw a stable-boy, a saddle on each shoulder, walking towards the main castle gate. The boy stopped walking suddenly and stared down at the moat. He edged closer to the water and then dropped the saddles.

Übung 3: Wählen Sie die richtige Antwort aus!

1. Where would you like to live?
   a) ☐ I like to live in London.
   b) ☒ I would like to live in London.

2. Do you live in England?
   a) ☒ Yes, I do.
   b) ☐ Yes, I am living in England.

3. What is your name?
   a) ☐ Call me Queen Elizabeth.
   b) ☒ My name is Queen Elizabeth.

4. What day is it?
   a) [ ] Today is weekend.
   b) [x] It's Friday.

5. Where was the Queen born?
   a) [x] She was born in London.
   b) [ ] She is born in London.

The noise startled the horse and it whinnied loudly. The stable-boy turned and looked towards the forest.

"Who goes there?" he shouted into the darkness. He started to walk in the direction of the noise the horse was making.

Knowing his cover was blown, the man in black kicked his horse hard and emerged from the trees. He rode fast along the edge of the forest, his long sword drawn and glistening in the dawn light.

"Come back here," the stable-boy yelled, running a few metres after the horse.

But the rider disappeared into the morning fog. The stable-boy ran back to the moat and took one more look at the body floating in the water; it was held still by the thin layer of ice that had formed overnight. Then he ran across the drawbridge and into the castle.

Übung 4: Welches Wort ist das „schwarze Schaf"? Unterstreichen Sie das nicht in die Reihe passende Wort!

1. castle, tower, office, moat Burggraben
2. horse, dog, saddle, whip Peitsche
3. cook, stable-boy, servant, mother
4. gun, sword, knife, dagger Dolch
5. morning, Thursday, evening, afternoon

6. walk, run, hurry, ride
7. mountain, tree, forest, wood

"Sire, sire," the stable-boy shouted.

The cook looked up from his pot, greatly annoyed. "Oh, what is it now, boy?"

The stable-boy gulped in his breath. "Come with me, please."

He grabbed the cook by the arm and tried to pull him away from the fire he was cooking on.

"Let me go, boy," the cook protested angrily. "Can't you see I'm busy?"

"Sire, please," the stable-boy pleaded. "I've seen something terrible."

"After last night's celebrations, the only terrible thing around here is the mess all those nobles made, and all the work they make for me. Do you have any idea how hard it is to cook for so many people?"

"No, sire," the stable-boy replied. "But once they've seen what's in the moat, they won't have any appetite."

"Hmpf. Another dead bird? You remember the last one you rescued flew away from you as soon as it could."

The stable-boy frowned; the cook was always making fun of him.

"It's not a bird," he said. "There's a body in the moat, sire. I think it's the heir."

"You're not telling tales again, are you, boy?" the cook said narrowing his eyes. "You've got a bit of a history as a teller of tales."

The stable-boy shook his head, his long hair rustling like straw. "Never, sire. As God is my witness it's the honest truth. Please. Come quick and see, so I know I haven't imagined it."

"Oh, if I must," the cook said, dropping his spoon and wiping his hands on his apron.

Übung 5: Lesen Sie weiter und setzen Sie die Verben in Klammern in die richtige Zeitform!

The stable-boy (1. drag) *dragged* the cook by the hand to make him (2. move) __________ faster. The morning light (3. be) __________ brighter now and the cook was forced to rub his eyes a little after the darkness of the kitchen where he (4. work) __________ by the light of the fire. They (5. stumble) __________ across the drawbridge, their footfalls (6. thump) __________ the wood. The stable-boy (7. stop) __________ next to the two saddles he had dropped and (8. point) __________ down at the body (9. float) __________ face down in the moat.

"My God," the cook said, his breath coming in short starts. "Is it really him? Fetch a stick, boy, so we can turn him over just to be sure."

The stable-boy ran to the forest and came back with a long piece of wood. He handed it to the cook who got down on his knees and tried to turn the body over. The moat still had a thin layer of ice and this cracked loudly as he turned the body over. Edward's pale and still face looked up at him and he dropped the stick.

"We must tell his lordship," he mumbled.

The stable-boy and the cook ran back inside the castle and started waking the attendants, who in turn woke the residents of the castle, including Lord and Lady Fortisman. Soon, the main hall of the castle was filled with bleary-eyed people and there was much yawning and grumbling; no one knew why they had been woken up and the stable-boy and the cook were waiting for Lord and Lady Fortisman.

The noble pair came down the stairs followed by a group of attendants, including three young girls who were holding the long train of Lady Fortisman's nightgown. The main hall became quiet.

Lord Fortisman, tall and dashing even at this early hour, stood on the second to last step. He smoothed his beard, which had only recently become flecked with grey, and looked at the people gathered in the hall. He was an imposing figure. His height, broad shoulders and full round chest, gave some idea of the power of his physique.

ÜBUNG 6 !

Übung 6: Übersetzen Sie die Wörter ins Englische!

1. Schloss ______________________
2. Burggraben ______________________
3. Stalljunge ______________________
4. Zugbrücke ______________________
5. Schwert ______________________
6. Wald ______________________
7. Königin ______________________

"What could possibly draw us all from the depths of sleep at such an ungodly hour?" he wondered, stifling a yawn.

The stable-boy edged forward. His hands were shaking. He had never spoken to Lord Fortisman before and his tongue suddenly felt like the size of a saddle.

"Yes, boy?" asked Lord Fortisman. "Are you responsible for waking the whole castle?"
The boy nodded, his face turning red. The cook gave him a sharp elbow in the side.
"Yes, my lord," the stable-boy mumbled.
"Well," Lord Fortisman said impatiently. "What is it?"
"The…there's something in the moat, my lord. A body, I think."

Übung 7: Ordnen Sie die Buchstaben zu einem sinnvollen Wort!

ÜBUNG 7

There was a loud gasp from the assembled (1. opplee) __________ in the hall, as if they had all breathed in at the same time. They looked (2. dornau) ______________ at each other, trying to see if (3. nnyaeo) ______________ was missing. Lord Fortisman's face turned grey when he recognized the notable absentees.

"Where are Edward and Catherine?" he demanded.

One of Catherine's attendants stepped (4. orfdarw) ____________.

"I (5. codekkn) ______________ on Lady Catherine's door", she said, "but there was no response. I didn't want to (6. btsiurd) ___________ her, my lord. She hates being woken up early in the (7. gornmin) ___________."

"And Edward's tower?" asked Fortisman.
"I knocked, my lord", said Edward's attendant, "but there was no answer. Lord Edward also hates to be disturbed."

Fortisman turned to the stable-boy. "Take me to the body," he ordered.

The boy led Lord Fortisman outside the castle and across the moat. Most of the castle residents and guests followed them outside and their footfalls on the drawbridge were loud enough to make the birds fly from the trees of the nearby forest. There were loud shouts of horror when they saw the body of Edward floating in the green water of the moat and everyone gathered close to the water, staring and pointing at the body of the heir of Fortisman Castle.

Lord Fortisman fell back a few steps and was steadied by several of his men. Lady Fortisman fell to her knees by the moat and started crying loudly, swaying from side to side. Her attendants helped her up and led her quickly back inside the castle.

Lord Fortisman gathered himself and turned to the stable-boy.

"When did you find him?" he asked, his voice dry and hoarse.

"At the first light of dawn, my lord," the boy said. "And I saw a man in black ride out of the forest and in that direction."

He pointed to the west where, in the morning light, you could just make out the towers of Stoutham Castle. Lord Fortisman stared at the castle. His eyes narrowed and he snarled.

"Prepare my horse," he shouted. "Men, gather your arms. We will depart in ten minutes." He turned to one of his attendants and lowered his voice. "Go and fetch the pastor. Take Edward out of the moat and ask the pastor to examine his body. Edward has been murdered."

Übung 8: Ordnen Sie die Wörter zu sinnvollen Sätzen!

1. find you did my when son

____

2. must Lord the Fortisman tell we news

3. depart will ten we minutes in

4. man black the darkness smiled in the in

5. Fortisman knees her to fell cried Lady and

The men ran inside the castle to put on their armour and to gather their swords. Most of the castle guests didn't know what to do and stayed by the moat, not wanting to walk into the castle before Lord Fortisman. They spoke in low tones with each other, their voices producing a kind of hum that was just loud enough not to get lost on the wind.

"Somebody take care of Catherine," Lord Fortisman ordered. "Break down the door if necessary."

Lord Fortisman looked down at the body of his son floating in the moat. He sniffed loudly, grimaced to fight back the tears that were coming, and swore to himself that he would get revenge for this devilish act.

"Come, my lord," said an attendant. "We must get you dressed."

! ÜBUNG 9

Übung 9: Lesen Sie weiter und setzen Sie die richtigen Präpositionen ein!

Lord Fortisman nodded and allowed himself (1.) ______ be pulled back (2.) ____________ the castle. In his changing room, he put

(3.) ______ his finest armour and recalled the last time he had worn it. It had been well (4.) ______ twenty years ago. The battle then had been against the Stouthams as well and Lord Fortisman's younger brother William had been killed (5.) ______ the sword of Lord Stoutham. The brothers had never been close but it was still painful (6.) ______ bury young William. (7.) ______ vengeance, Lord Fortisman and his men had attacked Stoutham Castle and several noblemen (8.) ______ the Stoutham family had been wounded.

So the feud continued and not even the marriage of Lord Fortisman to the sister of Lord Stoutham, a year after that battle, could end it. Thankfully, the calming reign of Queen Elizabeth I had brought relative peace to the counties, especially those close to London. Lord Fortisman was not far from the Tudor line of kings and queens and perhaps in line for the throne if Elizabeth did not produce an heir. He was eager to show himself a peaceful man, as was Stoutham who also had ambitions of power.

Fortisman worked hard to play down his rivalry with Stoutham and sought a truce which, except for a few minor fights, had lasted almost twenty years and had benefited both lords who now enjoyed favour with the Queen. But now, with the murder of Fortisman's son, that truce was thrown out the window.

He took his long sword in his hands. The sword had been in his family for generations, with each Fortisman having carved their initials in the blade.

He felt great sorrow that his son Edward would no longer carry the sword on for the next generation; indeed, now there was no heir to Fortisman Castle, no son to continue this great line of lords. There was only his wild daughter Anne who seemed more interested in enjoying festivities than in family honour and duty. She was spending time as a court lady in London but it seemed not even the strict royal court could bring her into line as Fortisman had hoped it would.

Lord Fortisman gathered his men in the main hall of the castle. It was a grand room, with the walls decorated with shields and swords and large portraits of several generations of Fortismans. Over the main doorway was a banner with the black and gold coat of arms of Fortisman Castle and a roaring lion. Seeing the banner always inspired Lord Fortisman and now he roused his men.

"Fellow noblemen," he shouted, his voice echoing in the hall. "The sons of Stoutham shall pay for this murder with their lives. Their blood shall run into a river that flows straight to the fiery pits of hell." The men cheered loudly, raising their swords and shields in the air. It had been years since many of them had been in a battle and they were now eager to prove their bravery.

The men continued to cheer as they headed out of the hall.

"Wait!"

They all turned to see Lady Fortisman standing at the top of the staircase. She supported Catherine with one arm and the young girl, though clearly distraught, was trying to put on a brave face.

Übung 10: Wie lautet die korrekte Steigerungsform des Adjektivs?

1. The relationship between the lords is (good) ____________ now than twenty years ago.
2. Anne is (interested) ____________ in enjoying festivities.
3. A sword is (long) ____________ than a dagger.

4. William is (young) younge ________ than Lord Fortisman.

5. The Fortisman sword is (old) olde ________ than the current Lord Fortisman.

6. They woke up (early) very ________ today.

"My lord," Lady Fortisman began. "We can't be sure that this terrible crime is the work of Lord Stoutham. I beg you not to rush out and do anything in haste."

"My lady, I hear your words", replied Fortisman, "but who else could it have been? The stable-boy himself said he saw the villain riding in the direction of Stoutham Castle."

"That does not mean my brother is guilty," she said. "Why must you always think the Stouthams are responsible for anything bad that happens here?"

"It could be just a trick, my lord," said Catherine, pulling herself out from under Lady Fortisman's arm. She ran down the stairs and crossed the hall, falling at the feet of Lord Fortisman.

"My lord", she continued, her voice breaking, "this hurts me just as much as it hurts you, but please, listen to the good lady. She is wise beyond her years."

Lord Fortisman patted Catherine's head with a gloved hand. "She is surely wise", he said, "but such words make one wonder where her allegiances lie."

Logalität

ÜBUNG 11 !

Übung 11: Bilden Sie aus dem Adjektiv ein Adverb!

1. slow slowly ________
2. loud loudly ________

3. quick quicker

4. sad ly

5. angry ily

6. hard hard

7. thin thinly

Lady Fortisman came down the stairs slowly. “It’s not only your son who has died today,” she said, her voice low as she tried to control her emotions and her anger. “Since our marriage, my allegiance has always been to you and this castle. But you can’t throw away a truce you have worked so hard to maintain just because of what one simple stable-boy saw. What will the Queen say when she hears of you attacking Stoutham Castle?”

“Edward is dead,” Fortisman shouted in reply. “If Lord Stoutham is responsible, then he must pay for his evil acts.”

“And when he’s not responsible but you kill him anyway, then what?”

Lord Fortisman opened his mouth to speak but no words came out. His wife was standing in front of him now and Catherine, still sitting at his feet, looked up at him with eyes so full of sorrow that they almost brought him to tears.

Übung 12: Welche Gegensätze gehören zusammen? Tragen Sie die richtige Ziffer ein!

! ÜBUNG 12

1. light	☐ awake
2. alive	☐ dusk
3. dawn	☐ quiet

4. asleep	☐ dead
5. loud	☐ long
6. short	☐ dark

"Ride to Stoutham Castle if you must", Lady Fortisman said, her voice sad and pleading, "but leave your weapons behind. Go in goodwill. Confront Lord Stoutham and see how he responds. I know my brother has made poor decisions in the past, but remember he inherited this feud, as you did. You fight the battles of your ancestors when I know both of you are good men with good hearts."

"And what of William? Lord Stoutham cut him down too." Lord Fortisman was still seething.

Lady Fortisman smiled thinly.

"William was always looking for trouble, you know that. And those battles were only ever a show of strength and power – goodness, you could almost call it sport – but William took it too far. My brother had no choice but to defend himself, as you would have done in the same situation. And besides", she added coldly, "you got your revenge."

"Our attack on Stoutham Castle showed that they are no match for the Fortismans."

"You went with the noblemen of four castles," Lady Fortisman replied.

She normally hated to argue with her husband and knew it was wrong of her to fight with him in front of his men, but she was sick of him always blaming the Stouthams for everything that went wrong. But when she was honest with herself, her brother did the same. She thought sometimes the two men behaved like children; in a different situation, they may have been the best of friends and not the worst of enemies.

Übung 13. Lesen Sie weiter und finden Sie ein Synonym zu den Wörtern in Klammern!

"I have made the (1. correct) ______________ alliances," Fortisman said proudly. "There are (2. a lot of) ______________ noblemen in our county who are more than willing to ride into battle with the Fortismans."

The men (3. shouted happily) ________________ loudly. Lady Fortisman stared defiantly at her husband.

"And that attack brought peace in the end," Fortisman went on. "William may have been aggressive and often (4. eager) ________________ for battle but his death did bring peace. We can't ignore that sacrifice."

"Hah. You still want to turn your bloodthirsty brother into a martyr, don't you?"

"It was an honourable death", Fortisman said, looking at his wife with cold eyes, (5. enraged) ______________ by her disrespect, "on the field of battle. He died with honour. Edward was (6. killed) _______________ in cold blood."

"Please, my lord," Lady Fortisman said, speaking more softly now, already tired of the argument.
"Do not act without good reason. If my brother is the murderer then strike him down, but give him a chance to prove his innocence, as

you would demand if he blamed you for a murder you did not commit."

Fortisman stroked his beard and pondered this. His wife was right. It would be very damaging for him to ride to Stoutham Castle with weapons drawn without good reason. And he too would not like to be held responsible for a crime he did not commit. He dramatically pulled out his sword and handed it to his attendant. The other noblemen did the same.

"We shall listen to the good lady's words this dark day," he said. "No more blood shall be shed today."

Lady Fortisman smiled and then bent over to kiss her husband's cheek.

"My allegiance is never in question," she said quietly. "And I expect you to take revenge for Edward's death, but only to strike the man who is truly the murderer. Killing an innocent man would ruin the Fortisman name forever."

Fortisman smiled thinly in return and bent down to help Catherine to her feet. Her face was wet with tears and her makeup ran down her cheeks in streaks.

"Be strong, Catherine," he said, gripping her thin shoulders with his hands and shaking her slightly. "We'll find the villain. And we will bring him to justice."

He turned and led the men out of the hall. Catherine fell into Lady Fortisman's arms and wept loudly.

A few minutes later the men rode across the drawbridge, their horses blowing big clouds of steam against the morning cold. Fortisman raised a hand for the men to stop when he saw Pastor Matthew standing by the moat with several of his servants. They had managed to pull Edward's body from the water and had laid it on the ground next to the moat. The pastor was cautiously examining it.

Übung 14: Beantworten Sie die Fragen zum Text!

1. Who is dead?

___

2. Where was the body found?

___

3. Who found the body?

___

4. Who does Lord Fortisman think the killer is?

___

5. What is the relationship between Lady Fortisman and Lord Stoutham?

___

"Good morning, my lord," said the pastor softly, looking up at Lord Fortisman seated on his enormous horse. "Though only a pious man like myself could call such a morning good."
"Your thoughts, please," Fortisman said softly, his voice almost lost on the wind. "Any sign of wounds or blows to the head?"
The pastor stopped his examination, stood up and walked over to Fortisman.
"At first glance, it seems not," he said. "Perhaps the young lord was pushed from his tower window."
All the men looked up at the tower. It was a long way down to the relatively shallow moat below and few of them thought Edward would have survived the fall.

"But that would mean it was done by someone in the castle," Fortisman said.

The pastor nodded gravely. "Unless he was killed outside the castle and the murderers threw his body in the moat." He cleared his throat loudly. "I'll need to examine the body more closely inside and inform you later."

"Come to my chamber when I return," Fortisman ordered.

The pastor nodded and then looked at the men on their horses.

ÜBUNG 15 !

Übung 15: Lesen Sie weiter und setzen Sie die passenden Wörter in die Lücken ein!

(support, religious, battle, rival, response, reaction, audience)

"Where are you heading with such a burly group of noblemen?" he asked. "Though they are unarmed, I see."

"I'm going to demand an (1.) ____________ with Lord Stoutham, to find out if he is responsible for this murder."

The pastor frowned. "Your (2.) ____________ has never been one to give straight answers to such direct questions," he mused. "Do you really think he will give you an honest (3.) ______________?"

Lord Fortisman sniffed loudly at the air, angry at the pastor's lack of (4.) ____________. His horse seemed to sense his anger and jumped a little, almost throwing him off.

"I believe his (5.) ____________ will prove his innocence or guilt, not his words," he said as he steadied his horse.

"Indeed. Men are rather terrible at hiding their true feelings."

"Wish us well, Pastor. We do not seek (6.) ____________ today, only truth."

"That's all well and good, but please be careful not to let your (7.) ______________ differences come between you and Lord Stoutham again. He may be a Catholic, but that does not mark him a murderer."

"Good Queen Elizabeth has ended that discussion," replied Lord Fortisman. "There will be no more religious battles. I respect the settlement that has been reached by Her Majesty."

"That may make things easier," the pastor replied, though it was hard to tell what he really thought about the subject. In truth, he did not stand behind the Oath of Supremacy, introduced by the Queen as the resolution to the problems between Protestants and Catholics. All Catholics in public and church office were forced to take the oath and many Catholic noblemen had already taken it as well, knowing that it would benefit their standing in the royal courts of London.

The pastor thought that such an oath would only cause more conflict. Religion remained a problem because all of the recent monarchs had had different religions. Henry VIII had been Catholic, Edward VI Protestant, Mary I a staunch Catholic who had persecuted Protestants, and now Elizabeth I who was Protestant. Who knew what religion the next monarch would have?

"But this isn't a religious concern," Fortisman said, snapping the pastor from his thoughts. "I only want to find the murderer who killed my son."

“Don’t be surprised if the murderer isn’t at Stoutham Castle,” the pastor replied. “I pray you to keep an open mind. Do not judge Lord Stoutham unfairly.”

“We go in peace this dark morning,” Fortisman said. “We have already seen enough death for one day.”

“Then I wish you well”, the pastor said forcing a smile, “and ask you to greet Lord Stoutham for me. I hear he’s starting to attend the Anglican services on Sundays.”

“If he’s not the villain behind the murder of my son”, Fortisman replied hotly, “then I’ll greet him for you.”

“This murder hurts you, and well it should”, the pastor said, his voice calm and even, “but if you enter Lord Stoutham’s castle with anger and rage, you won’t be received well. I beseech you not to act rashly.”

“You speak wisely, Pastor, as always,” Fortisman said, his voice calmer now. The pastor had the gift of being able to calm him just with the tone of his voice. “But I fear I’ll explode with anger if Lord Stoutham is behind this foul act.”

“Keep your anger inside you,” the pastor advised. “Keep it ready for when you’re sure you have found the villain responsible for Edward’s death. And remember that only a fool or a lover acts with his heart and not with his head.”

ÜBUNG 16 !

Übung 16: Welche Übersetzung enthält die richtige Zeitform? Kreuzen Sie an!

1. Ich habe ihn gestern gesehen.
   a) ☐ I saw him yesterday.
   b) ☐ I have seen him yesterday.
   c) ☐ I see him yesterday.

2. Dieser Mord nimmt mich sehr mit.
   a) ☐ This murder is hurting me deeply.
   b) ☐ This murder hurts me deeply.
   c) ☐ This murder hurted me deeply.

3. Für einen Tag haben wir genug Todesfälle erlebt.
   a) ☐ We have seen enough death for one day.
   b) ☐ We will see enough death for one day.
   c) ☐ We see enough death for one day.

Fortisman nodded and then took one last look at the body of his son lying on the ground. Edward's face was tinged blue, his lips pale, and the expression on his face was as if he had just swallowed something that tasted horrible.
Fortisman thought of the previous evening and the great feast they had enjoyed, celebrating the announcement of the marriage between Edward and Catherine. The happy couple had danced all night, spinning around in circles with the other dancers until they had all fallen to the floor in drunken laughter.
It had been a wonderful celebration and everyone had been so merry then. There had been a lot of dancing and singing and drinking, and they had all gone to bed very late. But before going to bed, Fortisman had been sure to check that Catherine was in her own chamber and not in Edward's tower as befitted an unmarried lady.
He sighed. Now, Edward lay sprawled on the grass and all that Fortisman was left with was anger and a burning desire for revenge. Last night's feast seemed to have taken place in another life.
He kicked his horse hard and the noblemen of Fortisman Castle galloped towards the shadowy outline of Stoutham Castle.

ÜBUNG 17

Übung 17: Beantworten Sie die Fragen zum Kapitel 2!

1. What was celebrated at Fortisman Castle last night?

____

2. Are Edward and Catherine already married?

____

3. Was Catherine in Edward's tower last night?

____

4. Who is Anne and where is she?

____

5. Who convinces Lord Fortisman to ride to Stoutham Castle unarmed?

____

Chapter 3: The Rival's Castle

They rode alongside the forest and through the mist. Fortisman could only think of his son. Edward had been rather shy as a child and afraid of many things. It had been important for Fortisman that Edward overcome his fears; the family had been given this name more than hundred years ago because the first Lord Fortisman had shown exceptional bravery and courage in battle. *Fortis* was Latin for courage and strength but also meant luck and fortune. With Edward's death, however, a great misfortune had befallen the Fortisman family.

Übung 18: Unterstreichen Sie alle acht Adjektive im folgenden Textabschnitt!

The air was brisk against Fortisman's pale face. It snapped him from his musings and cleared his head. But he could not get the last picture of Edward, lying on the wet grass with his face twisted in pain, out of his mind. Still, Fortisman couldn't help feeling that it was good to be out riding his horse, to have the fresh wind against his face, the cold air invigorating him. It reminded him of earlier days, when he had often gone out riding with young Edward before breakfast, teaching the boy horsemanship and how to use a sword.

Simpler times, Fortisman thought, and Edward had shown such promise, both as a warrior and a leader. The boy had excelled at everything, even at music, and Fortisman thought his son was destined for great things. He certainly wasn't destined to be pulled out of the moat, murdered in cold blood.

They were closer to Stoutham Castle now and the noblemen followed Fortisman's lead and slowed their horses to a trot.

"My lord," said Sir Stalwart, leader of the Fortisman Fighters, as the castle's force was known. "Is it wise to ride straight up to the castle? If they're waiting for us then we'll ride straight into a trap. Perhaps one of my men could ride ahead to announce our arrival?"

Lord Fortisman shook his head. "I know it's a risk, but the element of surprise is most important on this occasion, Sir Stalwart. If they're ready for us, then we'll know they're the ones behind Edward's murder. But if they're surprised by our arrival, taken unawares, then that might prove their innocence."

Stalwart frowned. "My only concern is that you remain unhurt," he said. "Edward's murder has shocked us all but we still need to make the right tactical decisions."

ÜBUNG 19

Übung 19: Formulieren Sie die Sätze im Passiv!

1. Lord Fortisman kicked his horse.

____

2. No one announced their arrival.

____

3. They slowed their horses to a trot.

____

4. The guests are eating the food and drinking the wine.

____

5. The cold air snapped him from his musings.

____

Fortisman smiled. He had great respect for Sir Stalwart, and it was on this respect that their friendship had been built. Stalwart had come to Fortisman Castle nearly twenty-five years ago as a young nobleman who was looking for a stable position away from the bickering and politics of the royal courts of London. The two men, united by their passion for horses and hunting, had slowly formed a friendship, with Stalwart always respectful of his place.
He had also given Edward much of his military training, acting almost like an older brother. Lord Fortisman was sure that Edward's death had hurt Stalwart as well, though he was doing his best not to show his sorrow.
"You know me to be an honourable man, Sir Stalwart," Fortisman said. "If Stoutham is behind this cowardly deed, then I will challenge him to a duel. I will not kill in cold blood."

"Don't forget the good lady's words," Stalwart replied, keeping his voice down. "You can't ignore that since the untimely death of William, the truce has been good for you. Stoutham is powerful, both in the county and the courts of London."
"That makes no difference if he killed Edward," Fortisman said, his voice now a whisper. They were in front of the castle and a warning horn was sounding.

Übung 20: Unterstreichen Sie die acht Fehler im folgenden Textabschnitt! Wie heißt es richtig?

Fortisman look at the closed drawbridge, its metal framework rust orange, and then up at the moat. He half expected to saw Edward's body float there but was then surprising to see any large fish swimming in the grass.

1. ______________________________

2. ______________________________

3. ______________________________

4. ______________________________

5. ______________________________

6. ______________________________

7. ______________________________

8. ______________________________

Sir Stalwart nodded and then looked up at the towers of Stoutham Castle. He only saw an attendant dressed in a red and blue robe, the colours of Stoutham Castle. The attendant had the hood of his robe over his head making it hard to see his face.

“State your business,” shouted the attendant in a high-pitched voice. Lord Fortisman and his noblemen looked up at the tower. Two guards appeared next to the attendant as did the front of a cannon.

Fortisman held up a hand in greeting. “I am Lord Fortisman. I request an audience with Lord Stoutham. We come unarmed and seek no battle.”

“State your business,” the attendant repeated.

Fortisman breathed out loudly, incensed that a lowly attendant would take such a tone of voice with him.

ÜBUNG 21 !

Übung 21: Lesen Sie weiter und setzen Sie die richtigen Präpositionen ein!

“It is a private matter,” he said. “Not one (1.) ________ your unwashed ears (2.) ________ hear. My words are only (3.) ________ Lord Stoutham. I have not ridden (4.) ________ the cold morning mist to state my business (5.) ________ a lowly attendant.”

“His lordship is asleep,” the attendant responded, maintaining a rather snide tone of voice. “Can’t it wait until later?”

“My good fellow, we wouldn’t be here (6.) ________ this early hour unless the matter was (7.) ________ great importance. I ask you (8.) ________ wake Lord Stoutham. I’ll take full responsibility (9) ________ ending his beauty sleep.”

The noblemen of Fortisman Castle laughed softly. The attendant took his time to reply. Fortisman wondered if the attendant was talking about the situation with someone else on the tower, someone Fortisman could not see.

"Very well," the attendant said at last, again in that strange high-pitched voice. "Please dismount your horses and tie them under that tree."

He pointed towards a tree which had a long wooden fence for tethering horses under it. "Then wait by the drawbridge. It will be lowered once his lordship has approved."

The attendant disappeared from view. Lord Fortisman and his men walked their horses over to the tree and tied them to the fence.

Übung 22: Bringen Sie die Wörter in die richtigen Reihenfolge!

1. audience Lord with would an I Stoutham like

____

2. horses tree tie to your the

____

3. come weapons without we

____

4. with attendant someone else spoke the

____

5. Castle's red colours Stoutham blue are and

____

"What do you think, my lord?" asked Sir Stalwart in a low voice. Fortisman stroked his beard, curling the bottom of his beard with his thumb and forefinger.
"Difficult to say," he said. "They had cannons ready and someone on watch duty. The drawbridge was also raised but that's no surprise. It's still very early in the morning."
Reminded of the time, Fortisman yawned loudly and a few of the other noblemen couldn't help doing the same.

Übung 23: Lesen Sie weiter und setzen Sie die Verben in Klammern in die richtige Zeitform!

"The castle is always (1. guard) ______________, as Fortisman Castle is," Stalwart said.
"That's right," replied Fortisman, his eyes (2. widen) ___________. He was awake now. "Who (3. be) ____________ on watch last night? He must (4. see) ______________ something, especially if anyone (5. leave) ______________."
"None of these men, my lord. We were all (6. celebrate) ___________ in the main hall. Young Donald (7. be) __________ on watch but he (8. do) ___________ not appear this morning."

Fortisman pursed his lips. "We must talk with him when we're back at the castle."
"He could be dead. I can send one of my men to ride back and see."
"Hold that order for now," Fortisman said, his forehead furrowed in

thought. “Even if Donald is dead, sending a man back would make no difference. We need to stay strong in number, just in case Lord Stoutham tries something. We can fight with our hands just as well as with our swords.”

The Fortisman Fighters nodded. Some cracked their knuckles and hit their fists into their palms, eager for a fight and to show each other what brave men they were. Fortisman smiled, proud that his men were prepared, if necessary, to take on the Stouthams with just strength and spirit.

The drawbridge creaked as it was lowered, the rusty chains grinding and crunching loudly. A group of armed guards started to cross the bridge before it hit the ground on the other side. The same attendant squeezed between the guards and then stood in front of them. Lord Fortisman and his noblemen were surprised to see the attendant was a woman.

Übung 24: Welche Gegenteile gehören zusammen? Ordnen Sie zu!

ÜBUNG 24 !

1. smile	☐	brave
2. strength	☐	leave
3. stay	☐	frown
4. raise	☐	weakness
5. the same	☐	behind
6. cowardly	☐	strange
7. in front of	☐	lower
8. familiar	☐	different

“His lordship has been woken,” she said. She pulled her red and blue robe tightly around herself against the cold morning wind, giving a hint of her feminine shape hidden underneath. “He’s not at

all happy and I advise you to be patient if he's angry with you."
Lord Fortisman smiled, impressed by the confidence of the female attendant. She did not seem intimidated at all by the large group of men that surrounded her.
"I will bare his anger," he said. "My business is more important than a simple quarrel over rising with the sun. Though I assume his lordship isn't taking any early morning exercise in order to rid himself of the burdens of middle age."
The attendant could not stop the smile from crossing her lips, or the amusement from shining in her eyes. She had shared some nights with Lord Stoutham and knew firsthand how sensitive he was about his physical appearance and the extra weight he was gaining. She recalled the terrible argument with the court painter whose portrait of Lord Stoutham had been far too exact, with the Lord looking much like a well-fattened pig standing on two legs. If the painter had not escaped the castle, he would surely have been executed.

ÜBUNG 25 !

Übung 25: Setzen Sie die Verben in Klammern in die richtige Zeitform!

1. Lord Fortisman (speak) ______________ with the attendant now.
2. The noblemen (ride) ___________ to Stoutham Castle yesterday.
3. Lord Fortisman (look) ______________ for Edward's murderer.
4. Donald (be) _____________ on watch last night.
5. Sir Stalwart (live) ______________ at Fortisman Castle for over twenty years.

The attendant regained her composure. “I’d like to take your word that you’re unarmed, but I’m afraid we must search you for weapons. I mean no disrespect, but the Fortismans have a history of trickery.”

“As the Stouthams have a long history of honesty,” Fortisman replied. “But we both lie.”

“Guards,” the attendant shouted. “Search them. If they try anything, strike them down.”

“We will submit to this dishonourable search”, Fortisman said, “but it shows no goodwill on your part.”

“In the same position, my lord”, the attendant responded, “I’m sure you would do the same. Trust is something earned and requires more than just goodwill.”

Lord Fortisman allowed one of the soldiers to search him. He thought that the woman was exactly the kind of attendant he needed in his own castle, someone strong and forceful but with enough feminine airs to take care of delicate situations.

Übung 26: Welche Wörter gehören in die Lücken?
(search, recognize, outdated, garments, weapons, preparation)

“They have no (1.) ________________,” said one of the guards.

Fortisman was slightly concerned that he didn’t (2.) ____________ any of the men. He wondered if Lord Stoutham had strengthened the castle guards in (3.) ________________ for defending the castle.

“None that you found,” said the attendant.

“I would be more than happy to have you search through my

ÜBUNG 26 !

(4.) ______________", Fortisman smiled, "especially if you're more thorough in your (5.) ______________."

The attendant quickly looked Lord Fortisman up and down. "Any weapons I find, might be considered (6.) ______________, my lord," she said, a smile in her eyes.

Fortisman should have been insulted. If the attendant had been a man, he would have been within his rights to step forward and hit him. But he could not stop himself from laughing out loud at the nerve and wit of the attendant. Where could he find such a woman? "Whenever you would like to put that theory to the test", he said, "you know where my castle is. Now, enough of this enjoyable banter. Please, take me to Lord Stoutham. My news is very urgent."
The attendant led the way into the castle and Lord Fortisman watched for movements under her robe but saw none. Instead, once inside the castle, he looked around at the furniture and the interior decorations. He had only been in there a few times, the last time being when he and Stoutham had negotiated the truce.
He was surprised again to see how similar the castle was to his own. It had the same long walkway from the entrance, and the same main hall with the stairway at the end. It was as if the two castles had been designed and built by the same person.

! ÜBUNG 27

Übung 27: Wer ist wer? Ordnen Sie zu!

1. Edward	☐ nobleman
2. Concocto	☐ Lord Fortisman's son
3. Sir Stalwart	☐ Lord Fortisman's younger brother

4. William	☐ sister of Lord Stoutham
5. Elizabeth I	☐ pastor
6. Matthew	☐ sorcerer
7. Lady Fortisman	☐ Queen of England

"Where is he?" asked Fortisman, expecting Lord Stoutham to greet him in the main hall.

"He must still be rousing himself," said the attendant. She took her hood off and let her long brown hair tumble onto her shoulders. "His lordship is an excellent sleeper."

Fortisman and Sir Stalwart exchanged a glance. Both were thinking the same thought, that perhaps Lord Stoutham was sleeping well because he had been awake all night, having been at Fortisman Castle to murder Edward.

Sir Stalwart leaned over and whispered in Fortisman's ear, "Surely the stable-boy would have said he saw a larger man if it had been Lord Stoutham, my lord."

Übung 28: Bilden Sie die Kurzform der Wörter in Klammern!

ÜBUNG 28 !

Fortisman nodded. "Maybe it was too dark to tell. And sometimes (1. it is) ________ hard to know a man's size when (2. he is) ________ seated on a horse and wearing a large coat."

"Perhaps it was one of the guards then," Stalwart whispered. "I (3. did not) ________ recognize any of those men outside."

"Neither did I," Fortisman replied. "If Lord Stoutham has increased his number of guards then that can only mean (4. he is) ________ preparing to defend his castle, perhaps from an attack of vengeance from us."

"(5. I have) ______ got a terrible feeling about this, my lord. I suggest we leave at once."

Fortisman turned to look at Sir Stalwart and was surprised to see fear in the nobleman's eyes. It was clear he too (6. did not) ________ like to go out of the castle without his sword.

"Patience, Sir Stalwart," Fortisman whispered, wondering if his own eyes showed his fear. "I need to see Lord Stoutham's reaction for myself."

"Yes, my lord, but if they're stronger in number and armed, we'll be no match for them. Choose your words carefully."

Fortisman started to speak but his voice was cut off by the loud trumpets that were being played at the top of the stairs. A plump man, rather short, and dressed in a long red and blue robe that trailed along the ground, slowly came down the stairs. He had a thick beard, still dark and a head of very attractive brown curls.

The noise of the trumpets was deafening and Lord Fortisman was almost forced to put his hands to his ears but did not want to show disrespect. He noticed that Stoutham had dressed for the occasion and looked clean and very much awake.

ÜBUNG 29 !

Übung 29: Welches Wort ist das „schwarze Schaf"? Unterstreichen Sie das nicht in die Reihe passende Wort!

1. think, wonder, smell, believe

2. early, ready, prepared, organized
3. lord, attendant, lady, queen
4. guard, fighter, warrior, sportsman
5. garments, boots, outfit, clothes
6. aggressive, violent, shy, vicious
7. tense, nervous, stressed, happy
8. short, wide, tiny, little

Stoutham walked across the main hall with short, bouncy steps and stopped in front of Fortisman. They stood in the centre of the hall and were quickly surrounded by their respective noblemen. The atmosphere was tense, with all the noblemen sizing each other up. Fortisman felt almost naked without his sword. Why had he let his wife convince him to not take his weapon? Was she plotting against him? The Stouthams were so aggressive, always ready for battle, always seeking to take the advantage when they had it.
But they did have honour, he conceded, and to his knowledge, no one had ever been killed in cold blood like Edward had. William died on the battlefield and was buried a hero and both castles respected fallen heroes. Fortisman thought that the murder did not fit their feud. And what of the truce? he asked himself. Was this the first step towards a new and more dishonourable feud?

Übung 30: Unterstreichen Sie alle zehn Adverbien des folgenden Textabschnitts!

"Good morning, Lord Stoutham," Fortisman said as brightly as the day would allow. It was still hard for him to believe Edward was gone forever.
"This better be very important," Stoutham replied intently, his

voice low and a vicious snarl on his puffy face. "I take my sleep very seriously."
Fortisman looked intensely into the brown eyes of Stoutham, trying to see what the man might know. Edward was dead and someone had to pay for that. But was it really worth throwing away the peace he had worked so hard to maintain? He stroked his beard thoughtfully and saw again Edward lying on the grass next to the moat, his face pale and his lips blue. Yes, it was worth it. He would do absolutely anything to take revenge for Edward's death.

"Lord Stoutham", he began, "excuse me for waking you at this hour, but I have experienced a tragedy this morning and need your thoughts on the matter."
Stoutham sighed. "Has another sheep died? Are the foxes outsmarting the brilliant noblemen of Fortisman Castle?"
Stoutham's guards and noblemen laughed. Insulted, Sir Stalwart stepped forward.
"How dare you speak to Lord Fortisman like that," he shouted. "We will not stand here and take these insults."
One of Stoutham's men took the handle of his sword in his hands, starting to draw it from its sheath. Fortisman placed a hand on Stalwart's shoulder and pulled him back.

ÜBUNG 31 !

Übung 31: Stimmt die Aussage? Markieren Sie mit richtig ✔ oder falsch – !

1. Lord Fortisman is carrying a sword. ☐
2. Lord Fortisman has been to the Stoutham Castle before. ☐
3. Edward died yesterday. ☐
4. Lord Stoutham is thin and young. ☐

5. Edward was killed in cold blood. ☐
6. Lord Stoutham has insulted Sir Stalwart. ☐
7. Lord Stoutham is happy to see Lord Fortisman. ☐

"Forgive my men if they're tense," Fortisman said, working hard to keep his voice even. "The tragedy has struck them as well, but we haven't come here for battle, not unless you give us reason to fight."
"The Stouthams have only ever defended themselves against you aggressive Fortismans," Stoutham replied angrily, his voice echoing in the hall. "And now you march in here in the middle of the night, as aggressive as always, and ask me to excuse *and* forgive you."
"Lord Stoutham, I come in goodwill. We're all unarmed as I'm sure your attendant has told you. We honour the truce that has stood for so many years and don't wish to break it, but this morning's event has shocked us all and left us barely able to control our anger."
"What tragedy do you speak of, and why does it concern me? Is my sister well?"
"The tragedy has hurt her but she's not the tragedy itself."
"Then what is it?"
Fortisman sighed loudly, wondering to himself how he would get the words out.

Übung 32: Bilden Sie sinnvolle Wörter aus dem Buchstabenchaos!

ÜBUNG 32 !

"Edward", he began, his (1. ioevc) ____________ unsteady, "my son and heir, is dead. He was found this morning and I'm now searching for the (2. rrdmueer) ____________."

Stoutham was shocked. "That is (3. rilbeert) __________ news," he said, trying to be as sincere as possible, but everyone in the main hall could see it was an act. Perhaps he was genuinely (4. cokeshd) __________ but he tried too hard to show it. "What happened?" Fortisman grimaced. "He was found this morning in the castle moat." As he spoke, Fortisman could see Edward's (5. sesellfi) __________ body lying on the ground by the water. "I suspect he was pushed from his tower (6. dniwwo) __________."

"That is most unfortunate. I'm sorry for you, but why have you come straight to me?"
Then Stoutham's eyes went wide with anger and insult as he realized why Fortisman was there.
"You think it was me or one of my men, don't you? How dare you make such an accusation? Get out of my castle. Now! Noblemen, draw your swords and drive them out," Stoutham shouted in anger.
Fortisman stayed where he was. He had a sword underneath his chin and Sir Stalwart had one pointed at his chest, but both men held their ground as did the other Fortisman Fighters.
"We will leave", Fortisman said softly, "but your actions do not help to prove your innocence."
"Your son dies and you immediately think the Stouthams are behind it," Stoutham said angrily. "How do you expect me to react? This is the biggest insult I've ever received."
"With all respect", Fortisman replied, "a man, possibly the murderer, was seen this morning riding in the direction of your castle."

Übung 33: Formulieren Sie die Sätze im Aktiv!

1. The murderer was seen riding towards Stoutham Castle.

____

2. Lord Stoutham was shocked by the news.

____

3. The peace is being put to the test by them.

____

4. Lord Fortisman will not be spoken to like that by anyone.

____

5. None of the guards were recognized by them.

____

"Ha-ha-ha," laughed Stoutham. "A man", he said sarcastically, "who could have been the murderer, rode in the direction of my castle. Then of course, it must be me. What other conclusion could you make?" And then he shouted, "Get out of here, you dishonourable villain."

"Do not mock me, Lord Stoutham," Fortisman said, his voice low and vicious. "Do not make me attack this castle again. You may have some extra guards and a cannon or two but you would be no match for the force I could assemble."

Stoutham, sensing his advantage, stepped forward. The sword was still at Fortisman's throat.

"You may attack when you have reason to," Stoutham said through gritted teeth.

"Such talk makes me believe you don't value peace."

Stoutham leaned forward even closer so that only the sword was between them. Fortisman smelled his rival's flowery perfume.

"You're the one who has shown mistrust," Stoutham said. "I'm sorry your son is dead, and please express my deepest condolences to my sister, but you can't point the finger at me for every foul deed that happens in your castle. Now, get out."

ÜBUNG 34 !

Übung 34: Setzen Sie das richtige Fragewort ein!

1. ________ tragedy are you talking about?
2. ________ is my sister feeling?
3. ________ did you find the body? In the castle?
4. ________ are you going to stop blaming me for everything?
5. ________ do you think Edward was murdered?
6. ________ was the first to find Edward's body?

The two lords stared at each other. The point of the sword touched the skin of Fortisman's neck, almost drawing blood, and he was forced to walk backwards.

"This isn't the end of it," Fortisman said when he was at the doorway to the main hall. "I must take revenge for Edward's death."

"Of course you must," Stoutham replied. "The sooner the better I hope, because when you find the villain, you'll no longer have reason to be angry with me. And then you shall come crawling back here to beg my forgiveness."

"I'll do no such thing," Fortisman said angrily. But the door to the hall was closed in his face and locked. The guards drove them from the castle and though he wanted to fight them as much as his noblemen did, he ordered his Fighters to leave peacefully.

Übung 35: Lesen Sie weiter und finden Sie ein Synonym zu den Wörtern in Klammern!

They crossed the drawbridge and it was (1. very fast) ___________ raised as soon as they were on the other side. The men (2. walked fast) ___________ for their horses. Fortisman looked up to see the woman attendant standing on the top of the tower. She had the hood of her robe up again and from this distance you could not (3. distinguish) ___________ that she was a woman. Sir Stalwart brought his and Fortisman's horse over.

"We'll (4. return) ___________ for our weapons and prepare to (5. charge) ___________ the castle," Sir Stalwart said as he (6. got on) ___________ his horse. "I'll send some of my men to (7. gather) ___________ the noblemen from the nearby castles and we shall (8. put together) ___________ a mighty force."

Fortisman took his time mounting his horse, wondering if Stoutham would send out his guards the longer he stood in front of the castle. But he only saw the attendant; no other soldiers had gathered along the wall, no cannons at the ready, no show of strength, no preparations to defend the castle. Stoutham had not been shocked by the news of Edward's death, but he had not been happy about it either. And when Fortisman was honest, Stoutham had every right to be insulted.

Fortisman knew that to attack the castle without good reason would be a terrible mistake. He may soon have the chance to be the first Fortisman crowned King of England and then he could start a dynasty of Fortisman Kings.

He would, however, need another heir and Lady Fortisman was past childbearing age. He thought of King Henry VIII who had executed his own wives. In particular, he thought of Anne Boleyn, Henry's second wife, who was executed simply for being unable to produce a male heir for the king. It was a terrible thought, but he could, if necessary, have his wife executed and then take a younger bride to be his consort, one who would give him the necessary heir to continue the Fortisman dynasty.

ÜBUNG 36 !

Übung 36: Übersetzen Sie und enträtseln Sie das Lösungswort!

1. wertvoll ☐ _ _ _ _ _ _ _
2. Erbe _ _ ☐ _
3. königlich _ _ _ _ ☐
4. Beleidigung _ _ _ _ ☐ _
5. Angriff ☐ _ _ _ _ _
6. Misstrauen _ ☐ _ _ _ _ _ _
7. Krone _ _ _ _ ☐

Lösung: _ _ _ _ _ _ _

"My lord?"

"Hold your orders for now, Sir Stalwart," Fortisman said, staring at the castle. "Let me first talk with young Donald and seek the wise council of Pastor Matthew. Perhaps the pastor has learned more from examining Edward's body."

"With respect, my lord, but Lord Stoutham almost smiled when you told him Edward was dead. And when he realized you were accusing him, he shouted that it was an insult, but he didn't deny it. He's clearly guilty."

"His response was understandable," Fortisman confessed. "I did insult him by riding over here."

"You did the right and noble thing, my lord," Stalwart said. "Lord Stoutham is behind this murder, I'm convinced about that now, and he has brought in extra guards to defend his castle."

"You're right, but we can't attack the castle unless we're sure Lord Stoutham is Edward's killer," Fortisman said. "All we have at the moment are emotions and anger. Like the good pastor said, only a fool or a lover acts with his heart and not his head."

He kicked his horse hard and galloped down the road. Sir Stalwart and the noblemen followed, but they did not ride with the force and speed that they had on their journey to Stoutham Castle.

Chapter 4: The Conference in the Chamber

Lord Fortisman's private chamber was located in the east wing of the castle. It was a large room with long windows which overlooked the landscaped castle gardens. He found it relaxing to look out at the trees and the grass and to watch the gardeners work. He often spent long hours in his chamber enjoying the peace and quiet away from the normally loud and bustling castle.

He had a broad desk, a comfortable leather chair, and a long quill made from a peacock feather which he had had since he was a boy. In the corner was a cembalo and he played this, quite badly, on the rare occasions when he thought he was alone in the castle. On the walls were portraits of his ancestors. Now, he sat at his desk and looked at them, going from face to face through the generations, wondering what each Fortisman would have done in his situation. The Fortismans were known throughout the land as brave and fearless warriors and he knew all of them would have acted with force.

ÜBUNG 37 !

Übung 37: Welches Wort ist das „schwarze Schaf"?

1. private, peaceful, noisy, quiet
2. brave, fearless, cowardly, strong
3. loud, bustling, busy, deserted
4. respectable, trusted, dishonest, honourable
5. thin, bulky, fat, stout

His thoughts were interrupted by the loud knock on his chamber door. Sir Stalwart came in with a tall, thin guard who was still rubbing the sleep from his eyes.
"You wished to see me, my lord," he said, a hand covering his mouth as he yawned.
As much as Fortisman liked the privacy of his chamber, he also enjoyed having visitors. Sitting in the large leather chair with the enormous desk in front of him, he felt very powerful and commanding.

ÜBUNG 38 !

Übung 38: Unterstreichen Sie alle zwölf Substantive (ohne Personenbezeichnungen) des folgenden Textabschnitts!

"Yes, Donald," he said. "I'm sure Sir Stalwart has informed you of

this morning's events." Donald nodded, blinking his eyes to wake himself up. "You were on watch last night. Did you see anyone leaving the castle, or arriving during the night?"
Donald shook his sleepy head. "No, my lord."
"You were awake, weren't you?" Fortisman demanded.
"Of course, my lord," Donald stuttered. "The music and singing kept me awake the whole night. And I would never fall asleep on my watch, my lord."

"I found this in the tower," Sir Stalwart said, holding up a large jug. He ceremoniously turned it upside down and a few red drops fell to the wooden floor. Donald looked at the jug and his face turned red. "I…I don't know anything about that."
Fortisman's breathing was loud. He was so angry he almost blew out smoke and fire like a dragon.
"How dare you fall asleep on your watch," he roared, his voice so powerful he made both Donald and Sir Stalwart take a step backwards. "Explain yourself before I hold you personally responsible for Edward's death."
"My lord, please," begged Donald. "I'm very sorry. I don't know what came over me."
"Give me one good reason why I shouldn't take you outside and cut off your head myself?" Fortisman shouted.
Donald's eyes went wide and he was too shocked to speak.

Übung 39: Formulieren Sie zur Antwort die passende Frage!

1. He fell asleep on his watch last night.

____?

2. I found the wine jug in the tower.

____?

3. Donald's face turned red.

____?

4. He fell asleep because of the wine.

____?

5. He didn't see the murderer because he was asleep.

____?

"In his defence", Sir Stalwart said, "he does have an excellent record as a night watchman."

"Be that as it may", Fortisman replied coldly, "but you of all people should understand how costly one mistake can be, Sir Stalwart. Do I need to remind you of that?"

Stalwart's face went dark and he narrowed his eyes at Lord Fortisman. He had been fighting alongside William during the last battle with the Stouthams and Fortisman had ordered him to watch over his younger brother. Fortisman had never said it, but Sir Stalwart knew that the lord held him personally responsible for the death of William.

"It's human to make mistakes," Stalwart replied, his voice low and his anger bubbling just below the surface. "And sometimes things are out of our control. Then we must accept the will of God – however hard that may be for us."

Fortisman sniffed at the air and frowned, thinking that was a poor reason to excuse away mistakes.

Übung 40: Lesen Sie weiter und setzen Sie das richtige Personalpronomen ein!

Stalwart turned to Donald. "Who brought (1.) ________ the wine? (2.) ________ know that's not allowed."

"One of the servants of Lady Catherine," Donald said quickly, eager to redeem himself and give the blame to someone else. "(3.) ________ gave (4.) ________ to me."

"Yes, so (5.) ________ would seem," Sir Stalwart said, and (6.) ________ couldn't stop himself from smiling. (7.) ________ took an elaborate and rather fetching brassiere from his coat pocket and held (8.) ________ out to Donald. "I also found this."

Donald's mouth opened to speak but again the words did not come out.

Fortisman leaned back in his chair, folded his arms and turned to look out the windows at the garden. It was a gloomy day, typical of late autumn. Most of the leaves had fallen from the trees and several gardeners were gathering the leaves which were scattered on the grass.

"On any other day", he said softly, "I would find this conversation rather amusing."

"My lord", Stalwart said, a warrior to the end, always prepared to defend the men under his command, "it was only a small mistake, one which had terrible consequences, I know. But if Edward was pushed from his tower window, then there might not have been much Donald could have done. He might not even have seen it." He

turned to Donald. “You were on the east tower, weren’t you?”
Donald nodded. “Everyone else was at the celebration.”
“My lord”, Stalwart said, “I recommend every tower has a night watchman from now on, even during festivities.”

! ÜBUNG 41

Übung 41: Übersetzen Sie die Sätze ins Englische!

1. Dieses Gespräch ist amüsant.

____

2. Wer hat dir den Wein gebracht?

____

3. Geben Sie mir einen Grund, warum ich Sie nicht köpfen sollte.

____

4. Ich glaube, dass Edward vom Turm gestoßen wurde.

____

5. Die Musik hat mich vor dem Einschlafen bewahrt.

____

Fortisman nodded his agreement. He thought that Stalwart was probably right, that Donald, even if he had been awake, would not have seen the murderer. Still, he couldn’t let this terrible mistake go unpunished.
“Throw him in the dungeon,” he said softly.
Donald gasped and turned to Sir Stalwart for help.
“My lord”, the nobleman said, “he may be a fool, but when we attack Stoutham Castle, we’ll need every available man.”

Fortisman considered this. "We'll take him out of the dungeon when we need him. Then he'll be the first one we throw at the enemy."
Sir Stalwart continued his protest. "With respect, my lord, but…"
"That is all," Fortisman said pointing to his chamber door. "He should be happy that his head is still attached to his shoulders. Throw him in the dungeon, in chains."

Übung 42: Unterstreichen und korrigieren Sie die acht Fehler des folgenden Textabschnitts!

Stalwart throwing the door open angry and charged from the room. Pastor Matthew was waiting outside, reading from a prayer book he held in his feet. He luked up in surpraise as Sir Stalwart storm from the room clutched Donald by one arm, pulling the boy along.

1. ______________________________

2. ______________________________

3. ______________________________

4. ______________________________

5. ______________________________

6. ______________________________

7. ______________________________

8. ______________________________

"Ah, Pastor Matthew," Fortisman said looking at the open doorway. "Come in, come in."

"I hope I'm not disturbing you on this dark day, my lord."

"With luck, your disturbance will keep me from my thoughts," Fortisman replied.

The pastor shut his prayer book and entered the chamber, closing the heavy wooden door behind him. He walked around the desk to the windows and looked out at the garden.

"It's good to remember the fallen," he said solemnly. He searched the trees for birds and was disappointed when he saw none. It was a bad sign. The winter would come earlier this year and many of the birds he fed during the spring and summer months had already flown south. "But it's unhealthy to spend long hours thinking about how they fell and who should be punished for it."

"It's difficult for me to lose such thoughts," Fortisman replied sorrowfully.

"Of course, but to think evil thoughts and to forever plot revenge is damaging for the soul."

"Pastor Matthew, you have always advised me well. What council can you offer me now? Have you learned anything from examining Edward's body?"

"Yes, my lord. It appears he was struck on the head, perhaps with a candlestick or a wine jug. The wound is minor but it would have been enough to knock him out."

! ÜBUNG 43

Übung 43: Welche Bedeutung haben folgende Redewendungen? Kreuzen Sie an!

1. to know one's place
   a) ☐ to find out one's location
   b) ☐ to be aware of one's social status
   c) ☐ to find out where the meeting point is

2. a bad sign
   a) ☐ unclear whether to go left or right
   b) ☐ not a good omen
   c) ☐ to say the wrong thing

3. to throw something or someone at the enemy
   a) ☐ to launch an attack
   b) ☐ to play sport with the enemy
   c) ☐ to ignore the enemy

Fortisman's voice faltered as he spoke. "Enough to take his life?" The pastor shook his head. He was a small man, quite plump, but the numerous robes he wore made him look fatter than he was. He had an open face, with puffy cheeks and brilliant green eyes. Fortisman had always been struck by the pastor's eyes, that they were as warm and inquisitive as they were cold and cunning.
"I doubt it," the pastor said, his eyes shining. As much as he was a pious man concerned with matters of God, he was also intrigued by matters of science, physiology and logic. "I'm sure young Edward had inherited your excellent ability for withstanding blows."

Übung 44: Setzen Sie die Verben in Klammern in die richtige Zeitform!

Fortisman (1. smile) ______________ at the compliment. "The fall from the tower then?"

The pastor (2. stroke) ______________ his smooth chin. "We do not know for sure that he (3. fall) ______________ from his tower window. He may have been killed outside the castle and then (4. throw) ____________ in the moat. And we (5. see) ____________ before that men (6. survive) ____________ the long fall from the castle walls. The moat (7. be) ____________ deep enough."

"Perhaps he was drowned?"

The pastor smiled with his green eyes. "That was my reasoning as well, my lord. But this is all gruesome speculation and it hurts to talk of such matters. Didn't the night watchman see anything?"

Fortisman laughed sarcastically and angrily. "Asleep at his post," he grunted. "I've thrown him in the dungeon."

"Ah, no wonder Donald looked liked he'd seen the devil."

"I think the devil was with him last night", Fortisman mused, "causing him to fall asleep."

"A plot, you think?"

"Like you said, only speculation, and gruesome at that. I would hate to think that there were people inside my own castle who would kill my son. But Donald said one of Catherine's servants brought him a jug of wine."

The pastor frowned. "Interesting, but hardly unusual. You're well-known for always being hospitable during such festivities and make sure everyone in the castle, even those working, have a chance to enjoy the celebration. I've always admired you for that."

"Thank you, Pastor, but perhaps it was unwise to be so carefree," Fortisman said softly. "But who was to know the devil was celebrating with us last night?"

Again, Fortisman tried to remember all the guests who had sat at the table and danced in the main hall. He could see colours, the guests dressed in their finest robes and dresses, some in the colours specific to their courts of origin. He tried to picture the faces, smiling and laughing, cheeks shining with too much wine, and could not believe that any of them would wish him or his family harm.

Übung 45: Bringen Sie die Wörter in die richtige Reihenfolge!

1. Lord of become King might Fortisman England

___

2. the Fortisman very always well advises pastor

___

3. insulted by accusation Lord was the Stoutham

___

4. is Donald dungeon sitting the in

___

5. Sir tries defend Stalwart men to his always

___

"The devil is always with us", the pastor said, his voice just louder than a whisper, "as much as God is always with us. But it's up to each individual man and woman to decide whether to do evil or good. Sometimes, their judgement is influenced by those around them, like sheep being led to the wolves by an evil shepherd."

"I wonder sometimes how you manage to keep such a strong faith in God, Pastor", Fortisman said, "and in man, I might add. All around us are men so ready to commit acts of evil, and to be led in the wrong direction, like sheep, as you say."

“The important thing”, the pastor replied, “and perhaps the most difficult, is to exercise forgiveness. For many men, such a thing is beyond them.”

Fortisman wondered if the pastor was referring to him. “I could never forgive the man who murdered my son,” he said.

The pastor smiled. “To forgive is divine. You would be well-received in God’s kingdom if you forgave the murderer.”

Fortisman sighed and rubbed his eyes. How could he do such a thing? he wondered. He knew he could never let Edward’s death go without getting revenge, even if his wrath was one of the seven deadly sins which the pastor had always warned him about.

“Is it Lord Stoutham who requires your forgiveness?” the pastor asked. “What news from Stoutham Castle? You were brave to ride there without weaponry.”

Fortisman frowned. “Lord Stoutham was shocked to hear that Edward was dead and insulted that I thought he was responsible.”

“Wouldn’t you have been insulted as well, if the roles were reversed?”

“Probably even more than Lord Stoutham was. I dare say I would have challenged him to a duel.”

ÜBUNG 46 !

Übung 46: Welche Wörter gehören in die Lücken?
(politician, peace, convinced, window, killer, sensitive, attack)

The pastor smiled, remembering how (1.) ______________ Lord Fortisman was to public opinion and insult. Sometimes, the pastor thought, his lordship was more (2.) ______________ than nobleman.

"Did he show himself as the (3.) ____________?" the pastor asked. He already knew the answer, for if Lord Stoutham was the murderer, then the Fortismans would be preparing to (4.) ______________ the castle.

"Sir Stalwart was (5.) ______________," Fortisman explained. He stood up from his chair and joined Pastor Matthew at the (6.) ____________. Both men looked at the garden, hoping it would bring some (7.) ____________ to their minds.

"But you were not," the pastor said.
Fortisman was quiet for a few minutes and watched one of the gardeners collecting the leaves from the ground.
"I can't launch an attack on Stoutham Castle without being sure they're behind this evil deed. It would be impolitic and would enrage the Queen," Fortisman said at last.
"It's very wise to exercise such caution, my lord."
"But someone will pay," Fortisman said angrily, tired of the pastor's endless talk of forgiveness. "If only I could find out more about what's happening inside Stoutham Castle."
"Do you mean send a spy?" the pastor asked, his eyes shining. He had recently heard fantastic stories of a man named Francis Walsingham who apparently had a large network of spies both in England and on the continent and who was working closely with Queen Elizabeth. Though he did not sound like he was powerful in London, it was rumoured that Walsingham had a finger in many different pies.
Fortisman smiled as a plan started to form in his head.

ÜBUNG 47 !

Übung 47: Formulieren Sie die Aufforderung höflicher mit ***would… please!***

1. Throw him in the dungeon.

2. I want you to find him.

3. Get out of my castle.

4. Don't talk to Lord Fortisman like that.

5. Give me some wine.

6. Leave me alone, Pastor Matthew.

"Who would volunteer for such a dangerous mission?" the pastor asked. He looked hopefully at Fortisman, wishing he could be the one chosen for the task. All the talk of espionage fascinated him. Why, even the churches were supposed to be full of spies.

Fortisman's face, which had been pale and grey since he saw the body of his son lying in the moat, brightened and some colour went back into his cheeks.

"Send for Sir Stalwart," he said. "Tell him to bring Donald back to my chamber. We'll disguise him as a merchant, a seller of weaponry, and send him to Stoutham Castle."

"Clever, but is the young night watchman suited to such a task? He has already failed you once."
Fortisman smiled thinly. "If he fails this time, I shall definitely cut off his head."
"Well", the pastor said, used to his lordship's short temper, "that should be motivation enough."
The pastor walked to the door. He opened it but stopped as Fortisman spoke.
"Thank you, Pastor Matthew," he said. "Your wise words and calm temperament have been most helpful yet again."
"It's a pleasure to serve you, my lord," the pastor said and then he closed the door behind him.

Übung 48: Lesen Sie weiter und unterstreichen Sie die richtige Variante!

Alone in his chamber, Fortisman (1.) rubbing/rubbed his hands together. He (2.) looked/looks out the window at the garden. Edward (3.) had playing/had played there when he (4.) was/is a boy and Fortisman (5.) has watched/had watched from his chamber as Edward and Sir Stalwart (6.) have been fighting/had fought sword fights with wooden swords. The nobleman (7.) had been/had being an excellent teacher and Edward (8.) became/had become a fine swordsman.

"Oh my beloved Edward," he croaked, his throat dry as he held back the tears. "You grew up so fast and now you're gone." Then his voice became harder. "But with my revenge, I'll make everyone know the power of the Fortismans and that we're not a family to mess with."

ÜBUNG 49

Übung 49: Beantworten Sie die Fragen zum Kapitel 4!

1. Where is Lord Fortisman's private chamber located?

2. What kind of musical instrument is in the chamber?

3. Who was thrown in the dungeon?

4. Why was he thrown in the dungeon?

5. What colour are the pastor's eyes?

6. Who is sent to Stoutham Castle as a spy?

Chapter 5: The Spy in the Castle

They tethered their horses in the forest and walked the rest of the way. Through the trees, they could just see Donald sitting on a cart loaded with swords, shields and other weaponry. There was even a small cannon the weight of which the horse was struggling against. "The drawbridge is down," Fortisman observed, looking at the castle. "They would never do that if they were expecting an attack." "It could be just a trick," Stalwart said. "A show of strength, that they're not frightened of an attack."

"Perhaps. Still, it seems unnecessarily risky. I would never allow such a thing."

Übung 50: Bilden Sie aus dem Adjektiv ein Adverb!

1. strong ____________________
2. careful ____________________
3. thin ____________________
4. definite ____________________
5. hopeful ____________________
6. terrible ____________________
7. soft ____________________
8. defensive ____________________

Donald stopped at the front of the drawbridge. Two guards came out to meet him. Fortisman and Stalwart couldn't hear the conversation but both men smiled as Donald and his horse were led into the castle. The drawbridge remained lowered. A group of children ran across it with small wooden swords in their hands. They pointed towards the forest and seemed to outline the rules for a kind of game.
"Shall we go back to the castle, my lord?" Stalwart asked, fearing one of the children might find them by accident.
Fortisman nodded his head but did not move. He stared at one of the children, a young boy of ten or twelve. The child reminded him of Edward; he had had the same eagerness for games and had always been looking for adventure in the forest near Fortisman Castle.

"My lord", repeated Stalwart, "they're heading for the forest. We cannot let them see us."
"Of course, Sir Stalwart. Lead the way."

ÜBUNG 51 !

Übung 51: Setzen Sie die richtigen Präpositionen ein!

The two men ran back (1.) __________ their horses and rode (2.) __________ Fortisman Castle. Neither man talked (3.) __________ the ride, with Fortisman deep (4.) __________ thought and the nobleman knowing his place.

They were met (5.) __________ the castle courtyard (6.) __________ the usual attendants and servants.

"Send a messenger (7.) __________ the royal court in London," Fortisman said as he got (8.) __________ his horse. "Queen Elizabeth should know what has happened today."

"Shall the message include details about who the killer is?" asked Stalwart. Lord Fortisman stroked his beard and considered his options. He could mention the Stouthams as possibly being guilty, but Lord Stoutham had powerful friends in London and any unfounded accusations could damage his own standing. Perhaps he should wait for Donald to return, but the Queen hated to hear news second-hand or to be left out of developments. No, he had to send word right away.
"Say only that Edward has fallen and that we suspect foul play," Fortisman said.

"Very well, my lord."
"And when Donald returns, bring him to my chamber."
"Yes, my lord. I hope he returns in one piece."
Fortisman smiled. "I have a feeling he will, which means we will be able to take him apart ourselves."
Stalwart nodded to Fortisman and then crossed the main hall to give the orders to the castle messenger to ride straight away to London.

Übung 52: Übersetzen Sie die Wörter ins Deutsche!

ÜBUNG 52 !

1. cold-blooded ______________________
2. truce ______________________
3. horsemanship ______________________
4. unfounded ______________________
5. espionage ______________________
6. weaponry ______________________

Fortisman headed for his chamber, then stopped. He called over one of his servants.
"Go upstairs and tell Catherine I want to speak with her in my chamber."
"Yes, my lord."
The servant went quickly upstairs.
In his chamber, Fortisman sat down at his cembalo and pressed keys at random. He looked at the sheet of music he had last played. It was a sorrowful ballad he loved to play, mainly because it was rather easy, and one which Edward had hated.

“The whole castle turns black when you play that miserable old ballad, father,” Edward had said in that typically light and jovial way that was so unmistakably Edward. “It’s a miracle the watchmen don’t jump from the towers and that the cooks don’t cut their wrists with their knives.”

Fortisman had started to protest but they had gone over this topic many times before and Fortisman knew what the result would be. He kept his mouth closed and waited for Edward to make the move that was part of the routine.

“Here, father”, Edward had said, sitting down at the instrument, “listen to this tune.”

! ÜBUNG 53

Übung 53: Stimmen die Aussagen? Markieren Sie mit richtig ✔ oder falsch – !

1. Edward could play the cembalo. ☐
2. Lord Fortisman doesn’t miss his son. ☐
3. Donald is dead. ☐
4. A messenger has been sent to the Queen. ☐
5. Lord Fortisman is good at playing the cembalo. ☐
6. Lord Fortisman walked to Stoutham Castle. ☐

Then Edward had filled the chamber and the castle with a rhythmical tune that put a spring in your step and a smile on your face. And Fortisman had sat back in his big leather chair, tapped the time with his feet and smiled with admiration at the heir he had produced. Edward was charming, handsome, cultured, an excellent sportsman, and a fine musician, and Fortisman was a very proud father. He couldn’t help thinking that Edward was monarch material. He had even gone so far as to come up with an elaborate plot to

remove Queen Elizabeth and install himself as king. But he wanted to become king by right and not by force.
Now, Lord Fortisman tapped the keys sorrowfully, wondering if his cembalo would ever play anything other than sad ballads again. The knock on his chamber made him stop.
"Enter."

Übung 54: Finden Sie ein Synonym zu den Wörtern in Klammern!

ÜBUNG 54 !

The same servant opened the door and one of Catherine's attendants (1. came in) ____________ the chamber. Lord Fortisman did not stand to (2. say hello) ____________ her and remained seated at the cembalo. She curtsied, lowering her head slightly as a sign of respect. She (3. be dressed in) ____________ a simple dress but had a fine figure and a round, (4. nice looking) ____________ face that was still enjoying the last bloom of youth.
"My lord", she (5. started) ____________, "the good Lady Catherine is too distraught to (6. come out of) ____________ her chamber. She's sick with sorrow and asks you to (7. pardon) ____________ her for not coming down."

Fortisman nodded, quietly glad that Catherine was ill with sorrow. On the ride back from Stoutham Castle, he had wondered if she could have been behind the murder; that Catherine, of all the guests in the castle, was most likely to gain access to Edward's chamber. It was not permitted for unmarried couples, but couples often ignored that rule. Hadn't he when he was about to be married?

"Of course," Fortisman said. "Please send my warmest regards to Catherine."

He looked the attendant up and down and wondered if it was her brassiere that Stalwart had found in the tower. A smile crossed his lips. If it was, then who could blame Donald for not wanting to wrestle with this attractive young girl?

"Yes, my lord," she said curtsying again.

"Thank you. You may go."

She nodded, backed towards the door and then all Fortisman was left with was a light, flowery scent which smelled like the forest in spring.

"Servant," Fortisman called.

"Yes, my lord?"

Fortisman looked at the servant. He too would have had access to Edward's chamber – all the servants would – and Fortisman wondered for a moment if he or any of the others could be the murderer.

! ÜBUNG 55

Übung 55: Welche Übersetzung enthält die richtige Zeitform? Kreuzen Sie an!

1. Edward konnte Chembalo spielen.
   a) ☐ Edward could plays the cembalo.
   b) ☐ Edward could play the cembalo.
   c) ☐ Edward could playing the cembalo.

2. Catherine's Dienerin ist attraktiv.
   a) ☐ Catherine's attendant is attractive.

b) ☐ Catherine's attendant was attractive.
c) ☐ Catherine's attendant are attractive.

3. Als Edward ankam, hatte der Diener den Raum bereits verlassen.
   a) ☐ When Edward arrived the servant had already left the room.
   b) ☐ When Edward arrived the servant has already left the room.
   c) ☐ When Edward arrived the servant already left the room.

He cleared his throat loudly and the words came out with difficulty. "Tell Pastor Matthew to begin making arrangements for Edward's funeral. We shall have it on Sunday."
"Yes, my lord," the servant said. He went out of the chamber and closed the door behind him.
Fortisman stood up from the cembalo and went over to his bookshelf. He moved some of the large and valuable books aside and pulled out a small container. He opened it and looked inside at the grey powder. The container was almost empty and he grimaced at the thought of having to pay another visit to Concocto, the sorcerer who lived in a cave on the other side of the forest.

Übung 56: Ordnen Sie die Buchstaben zu einem sinnvollen Wort!

ÜBUNG 56 !

He poured the last of the (1. drweop) ____________ into a glass and then filled the glass with water. The powder dissolved. He looked at the (2. diiluq) ____________ closely, knowing the relaxing potion that was hidden in the (3. trsnapaenrt) ____________ tonic, then drank it. He (4. tsredegga) __________ over to his chair and fell into it, almost missing. Once seated, he stared at the cembalo and tried to (5. mbrremee) ____________ that last tune Edward had played. The (6. esotn) __________ began in his head and he could almost see his son seated at the (7. mecblao) ____________, picking out the tune with his long and slender (8. gresnif) ____________. Then he passed out.

The loud knock on the door woke him and he very nearly fell out of his chair. Edward's music was still playing in his head. He looked at the cembalo and almost told the boy to stop playing. But then he saw the empty chair and the horrible reality came back. He stood from his chair and smoothed his robe.

"Enter."

The door was thrown open and Donald and Sir Stalwart entered the chamber.

"Ah, Donald," Fortisman said. "Excellent. What happened?"

"Well, my lord", Donald began, looking at the floor, "there's not much to say really. The Stouthams looked at the weaponry but bought nothing. I told them I'd been at this castle first and that you'd bought many weapons, as if you had a very large army to supply."

"Very clever, Donald," Fortisman smiled.

"Thank you, my lord, but they were not surprised. Lord Stoutham himself said that the Fortismans were always preparing for battle."

"Curse that dishonourable vagrant," Sir Stalwart said.

"Curse him indeed," Fortisman said, smiling again, the effect of the drug still with him. "Go on, Donald."

"Yes, well, I told them that the Fortismans had experienced a tragedy this morning and they knew that but tried to act surprised. Lord Stoutham has a thing for the theatre, I'm sure your lordship is aware, but he's a terrible actor. He shouted how your lordship had accused him of being the murderer and jumped around and threw his arms dramatically in the air."
Fortisman laughed as he pictured his rival jumping around foolishly.

Übung 57: Übersetzen Sie die Verben ins Englische!

1. anstarren ____________________
2. anklagen ____________________
3. knicksen ____________________
4. verdächtigen ____________________
5. Grimassen schneiden ____________________
6. glätten ____________________

"He said some rather nasty things about your lordship", Donald continued, "things which I won't repeat here."
"No, you won't," said Fortisman, still slightly amused as he pictured the small and plump Lord Stoutham raging with theatrical anger.
"But I think Lord Stoutham knows who did it," said Donald, smiling at his own cleverness.
"Is that right?" Fortisman asked, at once interested and suspicious.
"Well", Donald said, his eyes wide and bright, "I asked him why the drawbridge was down when it was possible the Fortismans

might attack and Lord Stoutham had replied, 'Because the murderer is not among us.'"

"That could mean that the murderer was perhaps there but left early this morning," said Sir Stalwart.

"Or that the Stouthams have nothing to do with Edward's death," Fortisman added. "If they bought no weapons, then they're not expecting an attack."

"They could have already purchased their weaponry", the nobleman replied, "because they knew the attack would come. Why would they buy weapons on the same day as the battle?"

"Good point, Sir Stalwart. But we haven't learned much more. Throw him back in the dungeon."

ÜBUNG 58 !

Übung 58: Lesen Sie weiter und unterstreichen Sie alle 15 Substantive des folgenden Textabschnitts!

"But, my lord, I protest," said the nobleman. "He has served you well."

"That doesn't excuse the terrible mistake he made last night. Throw him in the dungeon, but no chains this time."

"Yes, my lord," Sir Stalwart said through gritted teeth. "But what actions will we take against the Stouthams. They have extra guards, they don't need any more weapons, and the murderer was seen riding to Stoutham Castle. They're clearly behind the plot to murder Edward."

"Don't worry, brave nobleman," said Fortisman calmly. "I'll get the truth from Lord Stoutham, and I'll get it straight from the horse's mouth. Tell one of my attendants to come in on your way out."

Sir Stalwart grabbed Donald, who was speechless, his mouth

hanging open like a dead fish, and dragged him from the room. An attendant came in.
"Edward's funeral will be held at the castle chapel next Sunday," Fortisman said. "Please send an invitation to Stoutham Castle for the lord and lady to attend." The attendant nodded. "And prepare my horse. I have a short journey to make, alone."

Übung 59: Welche Bedeutung haben die Redewendungen? Kreuzen Sie an!

1. hear something from the horse's mouth
   a) ☐ listen to a horse
   b) ☐ get the information from the original source
   c) ☐ hear something second-hand

2. have a thing for something
   a) ☐ hate something
   b) ☐ think something is ordinary
   c) ☐ like something

3. get away with something
   a) ☐ do something and not get caught or punished
   b) ☐ miss something
   c) ☐ lose something

The servant went out of the chamber. Lord Fortisman got out of his chair and went back to the bookshelf. He put the now empty potion container into his pocket, took one last look at the cembalo and then hurried out the door.
A servant was waiting with his horse in the courtyard.

"Is it wise for you to ride alone, my lord?" the servant asked. "After the events of this morning, it seems there are enemies all around us."

Fortisman looked at the servant. "How do you know that?" he asked aggressively. "Have you seen or heard anything?"

"Not me, my lord," the servant protested. "I was working in the kitchen the whole night. There was a lot of cleaning to do. Why, I was still awake when the castle was woken up, my lord."

Fortisman narrowed his eyes at the servant. "What's the word among the servants? Does anybody appear suspicious to you?"

The servant shook his head. "No, my lord. But one of Lord Edward's attendants said that Lord Edward had been most unhappy these last days." The servant lowered his voice. "There's talk that the young lord jumped."

Fortisman slapped the servant the face. "How dare you say such a thing," he shouted. "Edward would never have jumped. It was murder, cold-blooded murder, and if anyone says otherwise they will fall beneath my sword."

"That's only what I heard, my lord," the servant said, his left cheek turning red.

ÜBUNG 60

Übung 60: Setzen Sie die richtigen Präpositionen ein!

Fortisman nodded, but already his thoughts had turned (1.) ________ Edward and the rumour (2.) ________ his unhappiness. He wondered what could possibly have made Edward unhappy? The boy had everything, and was about (3.) ________ marry a beautiful young woman.

"Send anyone who says Edward laid hands (4.) ________ himself directly (5.) ________ my chamber," Fortisman ordered as he mounted his horse. "I will not have anyone (6.) ________ this castle damaging Edward's good name."

He kicked his horse hard and rode (7.) ________ the drawbridge and (8.) ________ the forest.

He rode fast, knowing the way and following narrow paths that had been made over time. He was troubled by the idea that Edward had been unhappy and wondered if it was anything that he had said or done. They had sometimes argued, but didn't all fathers and sons?

He tethered his horse to a tree at the base of a rocky mountain and continued the rest of the way on foot. He saw smoke coming from the entrance of Concocto's cave and headed in that direction.

There was no door to knock on, no bell to ring, and no servant to announce his arrival. So, once at the entrance, Lord Fortisman could only shout the sorcerer's name and hope he was there.

"Concocto?" he called from just outside the cave. "It's Lord Fortisman."

Übung 61: Setzen Sie die Verben in Klammern in die richtige Zeitform!

1. Concocto (live) ______________ in a cave on a mountain.
2. Lord Fortisman (ride) ________________ through the forest last night.

3. Edward (become) ______________ King of England if he hadn't been murdered.
4. Some of the servants believe Edward (jump) ______________ from the tower.
5. Edward (be) ______________ unhappy before he was murdered.
6. A servant (wait) ______________ with his horse in the courtyard when Lord Fortisman came from his chamber.

He looked into the dark and smoky cave but could not see beyond the first few metres. Disappointed, he turned to start back down the mountain, but a voice stopped him.
"Come in, my lord."
Fortisman stepped slowly and carefully into the cave, stumbling on empty bottles and broken jugs as he walked. He felt a rat squirm from underneath his foot and jumped back in shock. Fortisman tried to calm himself down and walked on even more carefully than before. The smoke thinned the further he went into the cave. The light became stronger and he could see the sorcerer working by the light of the fire over a large cauldron.
Concocto wore a long black robe tied in the middle by a belt made of snake's skin. He had long hair, thinning on top and falling onto his shoulders in long grey strands. He was slightly hunchbacked, from having spent so many years bending over his cauldron, and his face was scarred and lined.
The patch over one eye added to his mysterious appearance. Fortisman had learned many years ago that in order to make a particularly potent potion, Concocto had used one of his own eyes.

Übung 62: Lesen Sie weiter und unterstreichen Sie alle elf Verben des folgenden Textabschnitts!

The sorcerer looked through his one eye at Fortisman.

"Are you here for more of the relaxant already?" the sorcerer smiled. "I felt a disturbance this past night. Did some evil pass through the castle of Fortisman to make you reach for the potion in a heavy dose?"

"Edward was murdered last night," Fortisman admitted. "It has been a difficult day."

He held out his potion container and Concocto took it in his long fingers. He filled it with grey powder and handed it back to Fortisman.

"I take it then", Concocto said, his voice airy and unconcerned, but his one eye shining, "that your men will gather arms and march on the castle of your rival."

"Only with due reason," murmured Fortisman. "But to be certain Lord Stoutham is guilty, I require another potion."

Concocto looked up, his eye locked on Fortisman. The eye narrowed and the sorcerer shuffled over to his shelf of jars and bottles.

"To seek the truth is a noble and worthy cause", Concocto said, "but to play with it like it's a game can be dangerous."

"All I want is justice," Fortisman replied. "If I hear the truth from Lord Stoutham, I'll be able to get my revenge."

Fortisman took a large pouch from the pocket of his robe and dropped it on the table. The coins jingled together loudly, almost spilling onto the table.

"Well, for such a valued customer", Concocto smiled, "I'll put my opinions aside and supply you with the potion you think will bring you closer to your so-called justice."

ÜBUNG 63 !

Übung 63: Welche Gegenteile gehören zusammen? Ordnen Sie zu!

1. full	☐ thick
2. safe	☐ entrance
3. narrow	☐ light
4. thin	☐ dangerous
5. heavy	☐ empty
6. exit	☐ small
7. large	☐ wide

He poured out a measure into a small blue bottle and put a cork in the top. With a small hammer, he forced the cork further into the bottle and then turned the bottle upside down to be sure none of the precious contents dripped out.

"I advise you to use this with great care," the sorcerer said as he handed the bottle to Fortisman. "Men carry secrets with them their whole lives that the world should never know, your lordship included."

Fortisman looked closely at the blue bottle and then put it in his pocket with the other container.

ÜBUNG 64 !

Übung 64: Formulieren Sie die Sätze im Passiv!

1. Concocto gave Fortisman a bottle.

____

2. Men carry secrets their whole lives.

____

3. Concocto is pouring a measure of potion into a bottle.

____

4. He turned the bottle upside down.

5. Fortisman dropped a pouch of coins on the table.

"Thank you, Concocto," he said. "But one last question before I go. It's possible that Edward may have been poisoned. Has anyone been here in the last few days to buy such a potion?"
Concocto walked slowly back to his cauldron and very carefully stirred the contents with an enormous wooden spoon, like a cook stirring a soup.
"I receive many customers", he whispered, "and sell many potions. I don't make men do the terrible things they do. I only supply them with the means."
"So someone was here?"
"People come and people go. Some come in disguise and others demand absolute secrecy. They pay well and I honour their demands."
"Don't make me draw my sword on you, sorcerer," Fortisman said, one hand clutching the handle of his sword, ready to draw it from its sheath.
Concocto continued stirring the contents of the cauldron. "It's unwise to attack a sorcerer whose powers extend far beyond the might and muscle of man," he said.
"Then name your price. If you know who killed my son, I'll pay you whatever amount of money you want. I must know who killed Edward!" Fortisman cried. He was barely able to restrain his anger and frustration while the sorcerer remained unnervingly calm.
"In my domain, money buys potions, not secrets. Good day, Lord Fortisman."

Übung 65: Setzen Sie die Verben in Klammern in die richtige Zeitform!

He (1. ride) ____________ fast through the forest, angry that the sorcerer (2. not tell) ____________ him anything. However, in saying nothing Concocto had said something. He (3. not deny) ____________ that someone had purchased a poison with the intention of using it to murder Edward.

Fortisman (4. know) __________ very well how costly Concocto's potions (5. be) ____________ and that (6. mean) ____________ the buyer had to have the necessary financial means to pay the sorcerer's high prices. So the buyer, the villain who (7. murder) ____________ Edward, could not possibly be a commoner; he would have to be a member of the upper class or at least a rich merchant. Lord Stoutham would have the means, Fortisman (8. think) __________ to himself, but how did he know of the sorcerer?

He turned his horse away from the direction of his castle and galloped south towards the nearest village. The local villagers bowed and curtsied when they saw him trotting down the main street. Some of the women even cried. It was just a small village but he liked the attention.

He stopped in front of a small inn, tied his horse and went inside. All the talking ceased when he entered and the men looked at him with sad and respectful eyes. Clearly, the news of Edward's death had already travelled to the village. The old innkeeper came forward. "You honour us with your presence, my lord," he said. "And let me be the first to express our deepest sorrow at the loss of Lord Edward."

Lord Fortisman nodded and then took the innkeeper aside. "You are one of the few who know the location of the sorcerer's cave," he whispered. "Has anyone come here asking for directions?"

The innkeeper screwed up his old and lined face and then looked down at the floor.

"I take it your silence was paid for," Fortisman said angrily.

The innkeeper nodded. "I can only say that you know the man who was here."

"Was it Lord Stoutham?"

"I'm sorry, my lord, but I can't say who it was. I have my honour as well."

Fortisman grunted. "You Catholics always stick together," he said, and then he stormed from the inn. He climbed back onto his horse. All roads of guilt were leading towards Lord Stoutham, he thought to himself. The truth potion would be the final proof.

He approached the castle at a gallop. The watchman saw him just in time and the drawbridge was lowered quickly enough so that Fortisman did not have to slow his horse. He rode into the castle courtyard where several servants rushed out to meet him.

Übung 66: Stimmen die Aussagen? Markieren Sie mit richtig ✔ oder falsch – !

ÜBUNG 66 !

1. Lord Fortisman got the potion for free. ☐
2. The messenger has returned from Stoutham Castle. ☐
3. No one saw Lord Fortisman riding towards the castle. ☐

4. Concocto has only rich people and noblemen for customers. ☐
5. Lord Fortisman went into Concocto's cave without his sword. ☐
6. The innkeeper knows where the sorcerer lives. ☐

"Has the messenger returned from London?" Fortisman asked as his climbed down from his horse.
"No, my lord," said one servant.
"Well, delivering news to the Queen can sometimes be a difficult task." He walked into the castle with several servants following him. "But surely the other messenger has returned from Stoutham Castle? Will those villains attend Edward's funeral?"
"The messenger spoke with Lady Fortisman when he returned, my lord. You weren't in the castle."
Fortisman lowered his voice. "Very well. Then I shall speak with her."
"Shall I announce your arrival to her ladyship?"
"I shall not go up unannounced," Fortisman said. "But I must first go to my chamber. It will only take a few minutes."
"Yes, my lord."

ÜBUNG 67

Übung 67: Setzen Sie das richtige Fragewort ein!

1. ____________ are you writing to?
2. ____________ news did he bring?
3. ____________ is Concocto's cave?
4. ____________ much did Fortisman pay for the potion?
5. ____________ will the messenger return from London?
6. ____________ doesn't Fortisman want to see his wife?

The servant went upstairs and Fortisman hid the potions on the bookshelf in his chamber. He took another long look at the cembalo and its empty chair before leaving the chamber and going upstairs.

The servant knocked on the door to Lady Fortisman's chamber, and it was opened by a young attendant whose eyes were red from crying. She curtsied to Lord Fortisman and stepped aside to allow him to enter. He saw his wife sitting at her small desk with a quill in one hand and a silk cloth in the other. She looked up at him and dabbed her eyes with the cloth.

"Leave us," she said. All four of her attendants quickly left the room, the last closing the door behind her.

"Are you writing to Anne?" Lord Fortisman asked, making his voice as soft and caring as possible; no easy task for a man used to giving orders and getting his way.

Lady Fortisman nodded. "She'll be stunned by the news," she said, her voice dry. "I hope she'll be alright and make it in time."

"If she leaves straight away, then it shouldn't be a problem."

Übung 68: Welches Wort gehört in welche Lücke?
(snakes, eager, together, stare, shock, furniture, letter, sheets)

Lady Fortisman looked at her husband with cold eyes. The power of her (1.) ___________ made Fortisman look away. His eyes moved around the room, taking in the (2.) ___________ he vaguely remembered, the bed where he had once slept (3.) ___________ with Lady Fortisman. When he saw the bed, he remembered how much he hated her thin bed (4.) ___________, that seemed to get tangled in your legs and arms as if you were sleeping with (5.) _______________.

"You seem rather (6.) _______________ to bury our son," she said at last in a flat, almost cold voice. "Can't it wait some more days? Then Anne will surely be here. You can't imagine what a (7.) _______________ it'll be for her when she receives this (8.) _______________. I have half a mind to take it to her myself."

"You're not in a fit state to travel, my dear," Fortisman said softly, trying to sound caring. He spoke to the floor, unable to meet his wife's eyes. "I don't recommend anyone to leave the castle."
"But you left."
"Ahem. I had an important errand to run," Fortisman stuttered. "One that couldn't wait."

ÜBUNG 69 !

Übung 69: Formulieren Sie die Sätze in der indirekten Rede!

1. "I have an important errand to run."

He said ____

2. "I will visit her in her chamber."

He said ____

3. "The messenger is riding to London."

He said ____

4. “You are not fit to travel.”

He said ______________________________

5. “I have not seen him today.”

He said ______________________________

6. “Delivering news to the Queen can sometimes be difficult.”

He said ______________________________

“Of course,” Lady Fortisman said, recovering herself and remembering how quick to anger her husband sometimes was. She wiped her face delicately with her silk cloth and spoke more clearly. “My brother and his family have agreed to come. That was a very noble gesture to invite them.” Then she looked at her husband from the corners of her eyes. “Or was it only a clever way to bring them here?”

Lord Fortisman cleared his throat loudly. “It was dishonourable of me to accuse Lord Stoutham so quickly,” he said, talking to the floor again. “I thought it might show goodwill to invite him to the funeral and to show that I don’t think he’s behind Edward’s murder.”

Lady Fortisman stared at her husband, trying to read his thoughts and know his true intentions. She knew he was a clever man, a man who valued alliances and honour. She also knew he had become a shrewd politician.

Übung 70: Finden Sie ein Synonym zu den Wörtern in Klammern!

ÜBUNG 70 !

“I want Edward’s funeral to be a (1. non-violent) ____________ affair," she said. "I don't want you and my brother (2. to fight with words) ____________ and insulting each other as you always do. I beg you to honour Edward's memory."

Fortisman (3. to grin) ____________ to himself. "We'll only talk. I have no (4. purpose) ____________ to argue or fight with Lord Stoutham."

Lady Fortisman nodded, but she wasn't sure whether she believed her husband. Nevertheless, she picked up her quill and (5. go on) ____________ writing to her daughter.

"Do you think Queen Elizabeth will (6. be there) ____________?" she asked lightly, (7. act as if) ____________ not really to care. Inwardly, however, she hoped the Queen would attend. It would be such a great honour!

"I'm waiting for a response from her," Lord Fortisman said. "It would be wonderful if she came but I wouldn't be surprised if there are more pressing matters in the royal court. There is her health, too."

"You seem rather eager to bury her as well," Lady Fortisman mused.

"Good lady, why do you take such a tone with me?" he asked, trying to control his anger. Fortisman couldn't help thinking his wife looked quite old slumped at her desk, her eyes swollen, her face red, her voice hard and cold, and the silk cloth held by a withered and wrinkled hand.

Übung 71: Übersetzen Sie und enträtseln Sie das Lösungswort!

ÜBUNG 71 !

1. Königin ☐ _ _ _ _
2. Streitgespräch _ _ _ ☐ _ _ _ _
3. Spiegel _ ☐ _ _ _ _
4. schlau _ ☐ _ _ _ _
5. Seide _ _ ☐ _

Lösung: _ _ _ _ _

"My lord, I mean no disrespect", she said, "but our son died today at the hand of another and you can only think of Queen Elizabeth and your standing with her."
"I think your grief is clouding your judgement," he said evenly. Moments like this, when his wife was so challenging and complicated, reminded him that the blood of the Stouthams ran in her veins.

Übung 72: Unterstreichen Sie die sechs falschen Verbformen des folgenden Textabschnitts und tragen Sie die richtige Form ein!

ÜBUNG 72 !

Lady Fortisman throwed down her quill and standing up from her desk. She still weared her nightgown and Fortisman is reminded of what a lovely figure she was having, a figure she had held into middle age when other ladies of her generation had been turning large and soft.

1. ______________________________

2. ______________________________

3. ______________________________

4. ______________________________

5. ______________________________

6. ______________________________

"You can kill all the men you want" she said, "but that won't bring Edward back."

"I can't let this violent act go unanswered," Fortisman shouted.

"And you can't show any weakness or sorrow either because the public might think poorly of you."

Fortisman sighed loudly. "Good lady, go to bed. Sleep away these mad thoughts."

She sat back down at her desk and picked up her quill. She put the nib in the ink well and then scratched it across the paper.

"I shall finish this letter to Anne before I descend into madness," she said sarcastically.

"Tell her to come at once," Fortisman said as he closed the door behind him.

"Yes," Lady Fortisman said to herself. "It will be good for her to see her father in a new light."

! ÜBUNG 73

Übung 73: Beantworten Sie die Fragen zum Kapitel 5!

1. Did Lord Stoutham buy any weapons from Donald?

____

2. Where did Lord Fortisman stop after leaving the sorcerer's cave?

____

3. Why does Concocto have only one eye?

4. What is Lady Fortisman doing when her husband visits her?

5. What does Lord Fortisman suggest to his wife?

Chapter 6: The Visitor from the Past

The blue bottle was just clear enough for him to see the potion inside. He stared at it, hypnotized by the slow movement of the liquid; it was much thicker than water and moved slowly and rhythmically. Sunday could not come soon enough for Lord Fortisman. He was sure his rival knew things about the murder of Edward and the thick potion he held in his hands would make Lord Stoutham tell the truth.

The loud knock on his chamber door almost made him drop the precious bottle.

"Enter."

A servant opened the door and a tall man wearing a black robe and a broad hat came in. Fortisman did not recognize the man and was feeling annoyed by the unwelcome interruption. Behind the stranger was a muscular attendant who removed the hood of his robe to reveal a shiny bald head.

"Baron Hoodwink, my lord," the servant announced grandly.

Hoodwink pushed past the servant and stood in front of Fortisman's desk. Fortisman stood to greet his surprise visitor and could barely believe his eyes.

ÜBUNG 74 !

Übung 74: Welches Wort ist das „schwarze Schaf"?

1. blue, black, metal, red
2. precious, valuable, expensive, worthless
3. cloudy, clear, transparent, translucent
4. servant, attendant, cook, king
5. rival, enemy, friend, opponent
6. solid, fluid, water, liquid

"Uncle George?" he asked. He hadn't said that name since he was a boy.

George had been the black sheep of the family and had hated living in the shadow of his elder brother. He moved away when he was young and accepted a baronetcy in the north of England. He had been all but forgotten, so much so that Fortisman barely recognized him. He remembered then that George was the son not of Lady Fortisman but of Lord Fortisman's mistress.

"I was in London," Baron Hoodwink explained, his voice like a dog's growl. "I came as soon as I heard the devastating news. It must be the work of the Stouthams. I'm here to lend my support in attacking Stoutham Castle."

"That's very noble of you," Fortisman replied, shocked to see his uncle now as an old man.

"When is the attack planned for?" Hoodwink asked, his voice pushy and demanding. "Tomorrow?"

Fortisman was taken aback by the abrupt manner of his uncle. "No attack is planned as yet," he said. "But I will march on Stoutham Castle only when I'm sure Lord Stoutham or one of his men is the murderer."

"You're delay just gives them the chance to make preparations for their defence," Hoodwink replied.

Fortisman started to answer but there was another knock on the chamber door.
"Enter."
"Good afternoon, my lord," said the messenger, red-faced from his ride. "I bring news from Queen Elizabeth."
"And about time too," Fortisman said.
The messenger, feeling all eyes on him, dramatically removed a scroll from his inside pocket and handed it to Lord Fortisman. Lord Fortisman unrolled it and began to read the Queen's letter.

Übung 75: Lesen Sie weiter und setzen Sie die richtigen Präpositionen ein!

ÜBUNG 75 !

"The Queen says, 'My dear Lord Fortisman, I have only sorrow (1.) ______ hearing the news of Edward's untimely death. Please accept my most warmest regards (2.) ______ you and Lady Fortisman and everyone (3.) ______ Fortisman Castle. The loss (4.) ______ your son and heir is heartbreaking and please know that all the members (5.) ______ the royal court feel your sorrow. And if it is foul play as you suspect, then we expect you to act (6.) ______ an honourable way befitting the proud Fortisman name. Unfortunately, matters (7.) ______ politics keep me in London, so I will be unable (8.) ______ attend the funeral. But I will be there (9.) ______ spirit. Stay brave, Lord Fortisman. Yours, Queen Elizabeth.'"

"Shall I also give the news to Lady Fortisman as well?" the messenger asked.

Fortisman shook his head. "Her ladyship is in poor health and shall not be disturbed."

"Very well, my lord."

"Thank you," Fortisman said. "You may go."

The messenger nodded and left the chamber.

"That's a shame," said Hoodwink, smiling with his eyes. "Perhaps the Queen is not so supportive of the Fortismans after all."

Fortisman frowned. "Will you stay for the funeral?"

"Of course, I've not only come for battle but also for mourning."

"Servant", Fortisman ordered, "take Baron Hoodwink to one of the available guest rooms."

The servant nodded. "This way please, Baron Hoodwink."

The man in black swept out of the room followed closely by his bald attendant. Fortisman unrolled the scroll and read it again. He wondered if his uncle was close to the Queen and had heard the news of Edward's death from a member of her majesty's court. Seeing his uncle now was like seeing a ghost, but he was quietly glad his uncle was in the castle. Baron Hoodwink was part of his family and was one more powerful ally willing to march on Stoutham Castle if need be.

He read the scroll several times until he fell asleep with the scroll lying on his chest, with the thin paper going up and down with the rhythm of his breathing.

ÜBUNG 76 !

Übung 76: Übersetzen Sie die folgenden Sätze!

1. Die Königin sendet ihre besten Empfehlungen.

2. Er las den Brief, bis er einschlief.

____

3. Sie schrieb den Brief mit einer Feder.

____

4. Fast ließ er die Flasche mit dem Trank fallen.

____

5. Der Bote überreichte Lord Fortisman den Brief.

____

In his dreams he found himself in Edward's tower. He was seated on a small chair and Edward was pacing the room, walking to and fro.
"Father, I want to go," Edward said. "All over England there are writers and poets changing our culture."
"A man of your breeding isn't fit for work in the theatre," Lord Fortisman replied. "Writing poetry has noble aspects, and the Queen certainly likes poems and watching plays but I shall not allow you to become some lowly playwright."

Übung 77: Welches Wort gehört in welche Lücke?
(heart, sarcastically, forever, words, laughter, mocking, geniuses)

ÜBUNG 77

Edward laughed arrogantly and angrily, and his (1.) ____________ hurt his father more than he wanted.

"You have no idea what the (2.) ______________ in London are producing," he said. "Men like Shakespeare and Marlowe and Jonson. Their words will last (3.) _____________."

"As will the Fortismans."

Edward laughed again. His (4.) _______________ laughter cut Lord Fortisman's (5.) ______________ in half.

"How can you believe that?" the youth said (6.) __________.

"People die, but (7.) ______________ live on."

"Edward", Fortisman said, raising his tone, "you're the heir of Fortisman Castle. When you become Lord Fortisman this castle will be yours. You may even become king if Queen Elizabeth doesn't produce an heir."

ÜBUNG 78 !

Übung 78: Ordnen Sie die Sätze zu einem sinnvollen Dialog!

1. "I bring news from the Queen."
2. "I'm afraid she must stay in London."
3. "Yes, my lord."
4. "Good afternoon, my lord."
5. "Ah, messenger, come in."
6. "That's a shame. Thank you. You may go."
7. "And? Will she attend the funeral?"

Lösung: _ _ _ _ _ _ _

"I'd rather live in a cave and write plays than die a bored old lord in this castle," Edward said.

"I will never allow that," Fortisman shouted. He couldn't help thinking that Edward thought he was that boring old lord.
"Everything's been given to me by right of birth," Edward said dramatically. He paced his chamber floor almost like an actor pacing the stage. "But I think it may be better to throw it all away."
"Do you mean you'll refuse your inheritance?" asked Fortisman, stunned.
Edward stopped pacing and looked at his father. His eyes were so rebellious, the look on his face so firm, that Fortisman knew the answer.

Übung 79: Welche Übersetzung enthält die richtige Zeitform? Kreuzen Sie an!

1. Er wusste von nichts.
   - a) ☐ He didn't know anything.
   - b) ☐ He hasn't known anything.
   - c) ☐ He doesn't knew anything.

2. Er könnte König werden.
   - a) ☐ He could became king.
   - b) ☐ He may become king.
   - c) ☐ He might have become king.

3. Die Königin hat keinen Erben hervorgebracht.
   - a) ☐ The queen hasn't produce an heir.
   - b) ☐ The queen hasn't produced an heir.
   - c) ☐ The queen hadn't produced an heir.

He woke with a light sweat. His body was stiff from sleeping in the

chair and it was an effort to straighten his back. He left his chamber and walked into the main hall. It was the middle of the night and the whole castle was deathly quiet. It was so quiet he could hear the torches burning.
He took one of the torches from the wall and climbed the stairs to Edward's tower. The flames threw shadows on the walls and it looked like a group of ghosts were following him up the stairs.

ÜBUNG 80 !

Übung 80: Lesen Sie weiter und setzen Sie die Verben in die richtige Zeitform!

The door was closed but not (1. lock) ____________ and he edged it open, the door (2. creak) ____________ on its hinges. He looked around the room, (3. see) ____________ Edward's unmade bed and his clothes (4. scatter) ______________ on chairs and shelves. He (5. see) ____________ the small chair he had sat in that time when he (6. argue) ____________ with Edward about the boy (7. want) ____________ to become a playwright. He looked around for the jug or candlestick that Edward may have been hit with but couldn't see one. Instead, he (8. go) ____________ over to the large desk which (9. cover) ____________ with pieces of paper and ink-stained scrolls.

He picked up one sheet of paper and began reading. Edward had written a play, a tragedy, about a young Italian nobleman who

wants to become a playwright but his strict father will not permit him to leave the castle. The young nobleman travels to Venice disguised as a commoner and becomes very successful.
Reading through the pages, Lord Fortisman could almost hear Edward's voice in his head saying those words.

Übung 81: Bringen Sie die Wörter in die richtige Reihenfolge!

ÜBUNG 81

1. can't wrote he play believe I a

____

2. London wanted Edward to to go

____

3. Fortisman killer found yet the hasn't

____

4. going was you I tell but I to forgot

____

5. will leave the allow to you I never castle

____

Lord Fortisman, holding back the tears, put all the papers together and put them carefully in the pocket of his robe. He almost jumped when the door behind him creaked open.
"Oh, excuse me, my lord."
"What are you doing up here, Catherine?" He looked at her and then at the large candlestick she held in her right hand, the candle burning brightly.

"I…I couldn't sleep," she said, her voice breaking. She began to cry softly, still standing in the doorway.

Übung 82: Welche Gegenteile gehören zusammen? Ordnen Sie zu!

1. popular	☐ joy
2. interesting	☐ contempt
3. allow	☐ unknown
4. respect	☐ forbid
5. sorrow	☐ dull
6. nobleman	☐ stained
7. clean	☐ pride
8. shame	☐ commoner

"This murder has shocked us all," Fortisman said softly, still looking at the candlestick. "I also can't sleep for Edward comes to me even in my dreams. You were the last to see him before he died, weren't you?"

Catherine blushed. "My lord I was not in Edward's chamber last night. I went to my own room with my attendants when the celebration ended. They will swear to that."

"Yes, of course, but you seem to know the way to Edward's tower quite well."

"We often sat in here together", Catherine replied, "but we were never alone. We always had at least one attendant with us." Then she blushed. "Edward liked to read his plays to me."

Fortisman felt the thick bundle of papers hidden beneath his robe.

"We had planned to go to London together after we were married," Catherine explained. "It was a secret. It won't happen now so I can tell you."

Übung 83: Welcher Satz enthält die richtige Bedeutung? Kreuzen Sie an!

ÜBUNG 83 !

1. show agreement with something or someone
   a) ☐ He nodded his head.
   b) ☐ He frowned.
   c) ☐ He shook his head.

2. express surprise
   a) ☐ His eyes were closed.
   b) ☐ His eyes narrowed.
   c) ☐ His eyes widened.

3. show embarrassment
   a) ☐ His face went pale.
   b) ☐ He blushed.
   c) ☐ His lips turned blue.

Fortisman nodded, as if he knew this secret already. "And how had you planned to live?"
"Edward said he knew people," Catherine went on, but she spoke without confidence as if she had had her doubts from the beginning that the plan would work. "Some people connected to the royal court, I think."

Übung 84: Unterstreichen Sie die neun Fehler des folgenden Textabschnitts und berichtigen Sie diese!

ÜBUNG 84 !

Fortisman smiled, wonders if Edward would have going to London and used the Fortisman name to became a suxessful writer. How damaging would that have being? Would the humiliation have kaused him to disown his son? He most sertainly would never have been able to take the throne with a sun and heir who is a lowly playwright.

1. ______________________ 6. ______________________

2. ______________________ 7. ______________________

3. ______________________ 8. ______________________

4. ______________________ 9. ______________________

5. ______________________

"It was my preference to remain here, my lord," Catherine continued. She sniffed loudly and her voice broke as the tears came again. "I don't understand why Edward was so eager to leave. But now he's gone for good. I can't believe it."

"There, there, young Catherine," Fortisman said. He went over to her and put an arm around her shoulder. "It's been an exhausting day for all of us. Go back to bed. We have more hard days ahead."

"Yes, my lord." She left the room and pulled the door closed.

Fortisman stood up and went over to the window. He looked down at the moat that was shining in the moonlight. It certainly was a long way down. He wondered why Catherine had come up to the tower just now, and with that heavy candlestick. Maybe she too deserved a drop of truth potion. He put his hands on the window ledge, his right hand landing in a sticky pool of Edward's noble blood.

"She could have hit him on the head with the candlestick and then pushed him out the window," he said softly. "But why should she do such a thing?"

Übung 85: Beantworten Sie die Fragen zum Kapitel 6!

1. Will Queen Elizabeth attend Edward's funeral?

2. What did Edward want to be?

3. Which three writers did Edward admire?

4. Who comes to Edward's chamber while Lord Fortisman is there?

5. Where had Edward and Catherine planned to go after their wedding?

Chapter 7: May the Truth Be Told

It was a miserable day, with dark grey clouds, and the heavy rain made the ground soft and muddy. The guests gathered in the courtyard and then walked together towards the small church that was set on the grounds of Fortisman Castle. Pastor Matthew led the procession followed by Lord and Lady Fortisman, their daughter Anne who was so distraught she had to be supported by several attendants, Baron Hoodwink and the rest of the guests.
Lord and Lady Stoutham were there. To Fortisman's surprise, the couple had come alone, having travelled from their castle with only

a few attendants. He was rather disappointed not to see that confident female attendant who had met him at the gates of Stoutham Castle two days ago, but quietly glad there were no guards or noblemen.

Despite Fortisman having warned his uncle that the Stouthams would attend, there had been quite a bit of commotion when Baron Hoodwink and Lord Stoutham had first seen each other. It was only the sombre occasion and Fortisman's intervention which kept the two men from fighting. The conversation with his uncle last night had left him watching Baron Hoodwink very closely. Hoodwink was convinced that Stoutham was Edward's murderer and yesterday had visited the neighbouring castles to build an army of noblemen ready to attack Stoutham Castle.

"Many castles have pledged their allegiance to us," Hoodwink had said to Fortisman last night in Fortisman's chamber. "They're awaiting your order."

"Why did you do this behind my back?" Fortisman had asked. He had spent much of the day examining Edward's room looking for clues but had found little except for a small green bottle which was empty and smelled terrible inside. Maybe Edward had been poisoned after all, but Fortisman had reasoned that the murderer would then had to have been inside the castle, a task that would have been rather difficult for Lord Stoutham or any of his men. He had shuddered at the thought that his wife might be plotting against him, willing even to murder her own son. He knew that she sometimes bought potions from the sorcerer, an elixir of youth or some such.

"Come now," Hoodwink had replied. "Don't tell me you fear battle as much as your father did? It's very noble to die on the battlefield. And we must make the Stouthams pay for Edward's murder."

"Yes, when they're guilty", Fortisman said angrily, "and I'm not in the least afraid to die on the battlefield. If you had been with us for

the last battle, you would know that first hand."
"I meant no insult," Hoodwink had said. "However, there are some special tonics which give a man extra courage during battle." Then he had reached under his black robe and had taken out a small bottle. "I've used this many times myself," he had explained. "It helps you relax and concentrate when the normal nerves of battle may cause you to make mistakes. When we attack the Stouthams, drink it. It will help you be victorious."
Fortisman had taken the green bottle and, when Hoodwink had left the chamber, had removed the top and sniffed it. Its foul smell had almost made him sick. He had then smelled the bottle he had found in Edward's chamber and couldn't help thinking they smelled very similar. But his uncle hadn't been at the engagement celebration and so couldn't have poisoned Edward. Perhaps it was just coincidence that the two bottles smelled the same, or maybe they were both courage potions and Edward hadn't been poisoned at all.

Übung 86: Setzen Sie die Wörter in Klammern in die Lücken ein!
(nobleman, garments, church, artist, robe, funeral, altar)

It was a long (1.) ___________ and, despite the numerous torches and fires, it was cold in the (2.) ___________. Edward's body lay on a table at the (3.) ___________. The servants had dressed him in his finest (4.) ___________. Fortisman wondered if Edward would have wanted to be buried in such clothes; high quality (5.) ___________ in the Fortisman colours. He had wanted to be an (6.) ___________ but would be buried a (7.) ___________.

The pastor made a long speech and the ladies cried, dabbing their eyes with silk cloths. The men sat quietly with sad expressions on their faces, determined not to cry or show any emotion at all as if the slightest expression of sadness was a sign of weakness. Edward's body was placed in the tomb with all the other Fortismans and the guests moved into the warmth of the castle dining room.
Fortisman thanked the pastor, "That was a nice burial service."
"Such compliments cannot heal my soul this terrible day," Pastor Matthew replied. "This unnatural death troubles me."
Fortisman nodded. "Me too. It's almost as if Edward's ghost is with me. Edward's body rests uneasily in our tomb. I think I might go mad unless his body rests in peace, and having my uncle here hasn't helped. He only talks of fighting the Stouthams."

ÜBUNG 87

Übung 87: Formulieren Sie die Sätze in der direkten Rede!

1. The pastor said Lord Fortisman was sad.

2. The pastor says he feares dark forces are at work.

3. Fortisman said he could not think of anything else.

4. Fortisman said he would find the killer.

5. He said that he was going to leave the following week.

The pastor watched Lord Fortisman with his twinkling and curious green eyes and wondered what kind of plan he had, if any, to find the villain responsible for Edward's death. He wondered if Fortisman had given up finding the killer, or was he just waiting for the killer to show himself?

The other guests mingled around them, talking in low voices and drinking from silver goblets, but it had none of the joyful energy of the celebrations normally held at Fortisman Castle. The guests seemed uncomfortable and sat uneasily in chairs or stood moving their weight from foot to foot unsure of how to stand. They had all travelled here to celebrate Edward's engagement and now they were attending his funeral. It was a terrible turn of events.

Übung 88: Stimmt die Aussage? Markieren Sie mit richtig ✔ oder falsch – !

ÜBUNG 88 !

1. Lord Stoutham is not at the funeral. ☐
2. Queen Elizabeth is not at the funeral. ☐
3. Edward was buried dressed as an artist. ☐
4. The pastor said nothing at the funeral ☐
5. The castle guests feel uncomfortable at the funeral ☐
6. Now that Edward is buried, Fortisman will forget about the killer. ☐

"It was very noble of Lord and Lady Stoutham to attend," the pastor said, hoping to change the subject. "And to come alone shows great faith, especially with your bloodthirsty uncle here."

"Perhaps", Fortisman replied, "but they could also just be rubbing salt into the wound, taking great enjoyment from seeing us suffer."

The pastor shook his head. "If you look for evil in men you'll sure-

ly find it, but don't fall for your uncle's old hate and rush to blame Lord Stoutham for an act of evil we can't prove. Admire him for the courage and goodwill he shows by coming here unarmed."
"Of course," Fortisman said. "Perhaps it is a sign of goodwill, as you say. Go and tell Lord Stoutham I'd like to speak with him in my chamber. If he's cautious, say that you'll be present."
"Yes, my lord." The pastor moved across the room and spoke with Lord Stoutham.

! ÜBUNG 89

Übung 89: Unterstreichen Sie alle zehn Substantive des folgenden Textabschnitts!

Fortisman watched from the corners of his eyes but turned away when Stoutham looked in his direction. He focussed his attention on the guests and, like all castle gatherings and celebrations, was surprised to see so many people he didn't know. And even worse, they were the same guests from the engagement party.

He noticed that Anne was not there and he guessed she was too full of sorrow and had retired to her chamber. In the corner he could see one of Catherine's attendants, the same girl who had visited him in his chamber, speaking closely with Baron Hoodwink. He was surprised not to see Hoodwink's attendant, who was always at his master's side.

! ÜBUNG 90

Übung 90: Setzen Sie das richtige Fragewort ein!

1. ________ is talking with the pastor?
2. ________ did Anne arrive?

3. _________ many people came to the funeral?

4. _________ was the funeral held?

5. _________ did the pastor say?

6. _________ weren't you at the party?

Fortisman thought there was something strange about a baron talking so openly with a lowly attendant and began to move in his uncle's direction. But he was cut off by Lord Stoutham and Pastor Matthew.

"Yes, Lord Fortisman?" Lord Stoutham asked. "The good pastor said you would like to speak with me."

"Yes, thank you," Fortisman said. "This way. We can speak in my chamber in private."

"There is no danger, is there?" Lord Stoutham asked.

"I keep no weapons in my chamber, and the pastor will be there."

"Excellent", Stoutham said returning the smile, "but even if we do come to blows, Queen Elizabeth will be happy to hear that a Protestant pastor came to the rescue of a catholic."

"My lords", Pastor Matthew said, "I ask you to leave those differences in the past and look ahead."

Lord Stoutham nodded. "He speaks wisely."

Fortisman opened the door to his chamber and led the two men inside, closing the door behind them.

"Something to drink?" he asked lightly. "I keep a much finer wine in my chamber than is reserved for guests."

"Naturally," Stoutham said looking quickly around the room. He saw no weapons, but to be safe, stood close to the door. "I'll have a goblet of wine. Will the pastor also drink?"

Pastor Matthew smiled and shook his head. He stood between the two men like a father between two arguing sons.

ÜBUNG 91

Übung 91: Lesen Sie weiter und setzen Sie die richtigen Präpositionen ein!

Fortisman went (1.) ______ the table behind his desk and poured the wine (2.) ______ his back turned (3.) _____ Stoutham. Quickly, he put a few drops (4.) _________ the truth potion (5.) ______ one of the goblets. He picked that goblet (6.) ______ with his left hand and walked over (7.) ______ Stoutham. But he offered the goblet he held (8.) ______ his right hand. Stoutham narrowed his eyes.

"Just to be sure", he said softly, "I will take the goblet in your left hand. I'm sure you would do the same."
Fortisman shrugged and tried to show that he would never be so mistrusting, but Stoutham was right, and Fortisman's clever trick had worked.
"To Edward," Fortisman said raising his goblet. "May his soul rest in peace."
The two men drank and Fortisman sat down behind his large desk. He wondered how long it would take for the potion to work and how long it would last. He watched his rival closely to see if there were any changes in his expression or behaviour.
"A nice drop," Stoutham said. "A little bitter but I like wine with a kick." Then his face went pale and he stared at the floor. "The only problem is, all this wine is making me fat. And this wine is not nearly as fine as you said it would be."
Fortisman smiled, amazed that the potion had worked so quickly.
"Are you wearing a corset to make yourself look thinner?" he asked.

Stoutham nodded, his face blank as if he was hypnotized. "Yes I am."
Pastor Matthew narrowed his eyes and looked from man to man.
"Do you sleep with your female attendant?" Fortisman asked, a big smile on his face.
Stoutham nodded again. "Yes, quite often. Lady Stoutham isn't interested in night-time sports. The Virgin Queen sets the standard now."

Übung 92: Unterstreichen Sie die richtige Alternative!

1. Wine is an alcoholic/alcoholical drink.
2. The pastor is a theoretical/theoretic thinker.
3. Fortisman is an honourable/honourably man.
4. The potion works extreme/extremely fast.
5. The trick worked very good/well.
6. The story sounds very good/well.

Pastor Matthew moved around the desk. "My lord", he whispered to Fortisman, "what have you done to Lord Stoutham? This is most dishonourable."
"Step back, Pastor Matthew," Fortisman replied angrily. "You're my witness."
"You have given him a truth potion," the pastor said. "Don't be surprised that I know of such things. I may also know where you got it. Clever you may be but I question your honour."
"I want the truth," Fortisman said, hissing like a snake. "Now, step back."
The pastor went back to his previous position, but this time standing closer to Lord Stoutham.

"Did you buy poison from the sorcerer who lives in a cave on the other side of the forest?" Fortisman asked. He sat forward in his chair, eager for the answer.

"No."

Fortisman was stunned by the answer. The innkeeper had said it was someone he would know. "Did you kill Edward?"

Stoutham stared into space and then shook his head. "No."

"Did you have him killed?"

"No." Stoutham gave his head a shake and his puffy chin made a flap-flap sound. He looked at the pastor, his eyes suddenly clear, and then around the room as if he had never seen the chamber before. "What words have I spoken here?"

"You have told the truth," Fortisman said softly, his disappointment and shame written all over his face. "Please accept my apologies for marching on your castle two days ago."

Lord Stoutham stood up quickly and threw the heavy chair aside angrily; he may have been fat, but he still had a lot of power in his body.

"How dare you give me a truth potion," he shouted. He moved quickly around the desk as if he was about to hit Fortisman but the pastor got in the way and held Stoutham back.

ÜBUNG 93 !

Übung 93: Ordnen Sie die Buchstaben zu einem sinnvollen Wort!

"This is the most (1. sidoonurhblea) ____________ thing you Fortismans have ever done," Stoutham continued. He (2. trsuggdle) ____________ with the pastor, trying to get his (3. srma) ____________ free so he could hit Fortisman. "Let me go, Pastor."

"My lord", the pastor said to Stoutham, "please (4. drenudnsat) ___________ that Lord Fortisman was greatly disturbed by the (5. hated) ___________ of his son. In his (6. grean) ___________ and sorrow, he perhaps (7. decta) ___________ without thinking."

"That may be", Stoutham replied, "but that's no reason to dishonour me, a second time I might add."
"Lord Stoutham, I'm sorry," Fortisman said. "But my stable-boy said he saw a rider heading for your castle on the morning of Edward's death."
Stoutham breathed out angrily and paced around the room, but he did not leave.
"You said that at my castle," he said.
"And you mocked me for it", Fortisman replied, "and in doing so, insulted me and my men."
"That insult was nothing compared to the dishonour of accusing an innocent man of murder," Stoutham said. He bent down and picked up the chair he had thrown aside and then sat down in it; he was a bit out of breath.
"My lords", the pastor said, interrupting Fortisman just before he was about to continue arguing with Stoutham, "I have an idea, one which might settle your argument, at least for now."
Both men looked at the pastor, prepared to listen.
"Perhaps Lord Fortisman can redeem himself by taking a drop of the truth potion," the pastor said to Stoutham. "Then you may ask him some deep questions."
"Now, Pastor, I don't think that's necessary," Fortisman said.
Stoutham rubbed his fat hands together. "It's an excellent idea." He picked up his goblet of wine and handed it to across the large desk to Fortisman. "Drink, and we shall be even."

Fortisman took the goblet and looked at the pastor who smiled and nodded his head. Fortisman took a long drink and then put the goblet down on his desk. He felt dizzy, and the room began to spin slightly; the effect was not so different from the relaxant drug he sometimes took to calm his nerves.

ÜBUNG 94 !

Übung 94: Formulieren Sie in if-Sätze um!

1. Fortisman finds the killer. He kills him.

____

2. Edward was still alive. He will go to London.

____

3. Donald had been awake. He saw the murderer.

____

4. You see her. Say hello for me.

____

"Why did you marry my sister?" Stoutham asked.
"It was my father's last request before he died," Fortisman said softly, his voice flat and even. "He wanted to bring the two castles closer together, to end the feud."
"And so it did. At least the truce has lasted for quite a while now. Did you love my sister?"
"No, not when I married her", Fortisman said, "but I had to honour my father's wish. And she bore me two children and has always been a faithful wife to me."

"What will happen if you become king? Mary's old now and can't possibly give you another child. Will you divorce her and take another wife as your consort?"

"I don't know," Fortisman replied.

"Do you hate the Stouthams?"

Fortisman shook his head and his eyes were clear. He stroked his beard thoughtfully and looked Stoutham in the eyes.

"Not now I know the truth," he said. "Do you hate the Fortismans?"

"I was taught to," Stoutham replied. He moved around the table and held out his hand. Fortisman stood and the two men shook hands.

"As long as I live, the Fortismans will never fight with the Stouthams again," Lord Fortisman declared.

"As long as I live", Stoutham replied dramatically, "it shall be the same. I pledge allegiance to your castle."

"And I to yours. It was very unfair of me to think you were responsible for Edward's death just because of our past disagreements."

"My lords", said Pastor Matthew, his green eyes shining, "I praise you both for ending your feud and for your honesty, even though it was given to you by a drug, but the matter remains unresolved. Lord Stoutham is innocent and we are no closer to knowing who Edward's killer is."

"But I heard that Edward was a fine young nobleman," Stoutham said. He sat in one of the chairs facing the desk and crossed his legs as if he had sat in this chamber many times. "Why would anyone want to kill him? Where's the motivation?"

The word "motivation" hit Fortisman like a hard slap in the face. It was the one part of the murder he had not considered. He had thought it was an act of revenge from Stoutham but he had been wrong about that.

"Edward was your only son and heir," Stoutham said, talking like he and Fortisman were old friends. "If you were to die, who would inherit the castle? And more, if you became king, which from what I hear from London becomes more likely by the day, who would succeed you?"

Fortisman thought of his wild and moody daughter Anne whose time in London had barely matured her. Then he remembered his uncle; George was someone he would know, someone also the old innkeeper would remember. He reached behind him and pulled a long rope. A bell rang somewhere in the castle and before the sound had stopped, there was a knock on the door.

"Enter."

"Yes, my lord?" asked the servant.

"Bring Baron Hoodwink to my chamber", Fortisman ordered, "and make sure he is unarmed."

The servant rushed out and the men waited impatiently in the chamber.

The servant returned, breathing heavily. "Baron Hoodwink's not in the main hall or the dining room, my lord. And his attendant is also missing."

"Aaargh!" Fortisman shouted in anger. "Send Sir Stalwart and some men to search the castle for him," he ordered. "Raise the drawbridge and keep it guarded. No one is allowed to leave the castle. And bring Catherine's attendant to my chamber at once."

"Yes, my lord." The servant rushed out of the chamber.

ÜBUNG 95

Übung 95: Vorsicht, „falsche Freunde"! Unterstreichen Sie die richtige Übersetzung!

1. sympathisch – sympathy, likeable, sympathetic
2. sensibel – sensitive, sensible, sensual
3. Art – art, material, sort

4. gültig – valid, guilty, good
5. kindlich – kindly, childlike, young

Fortisman filled three goblets with wine and gave one to Stoutham and put one on his desk. The third he filled with a large dose of the truth potion and then held that goblet in his right hand. He was surprised to see his hand was shaking slightly and almost drank from the goblet to calm his nerves, but stopped himself just in time. The servant returned with Catherine's attendant.

"Yes, my lord?" she asked, surprised to see Lord Stoutham sitting comfortably in one of the chairs, a goblet of wine in his hands.

"What's your name?" Fortisman asked.

"Pandora, my lord."

"Leave us," Fortisman said to the servant who left and closed the door behind him. "Lord Stoutham and I are having a friendly argument over this wine, Pandora," Fortisman began, his voice light and airy. "We have been calling in guests to taste it to see what their opinions are. Please try it and tell us what you think."

"Well, I'm not a wine expert," she said quietly.

"It doesn't matter," Fortisman said. "All the other servants and attendants have tried it."

"Yes, my lord. As you wish." Pandora took the goblet, drank and then put the goblet on the desk. "Bitter", she said, "and heavy too. My head is already starting to spin."

All three men watched as her face went blank and she fell to the floor. Pastor Matthew reached her first and lifted her onto a chair. He slapped her face lightly a few times.

"How much did you give her, my lord?" the pastor asked. "She's no longer awake."

"Clearly too much," Fortisman said, angry with himself. "But I thought a larger dose would make the potion last longer."

"Wait. She's waking up," the pastor said. He tried to hold her head steady but it kept dropping onto her chest. Her eyes were open but she was not blinking, and she just stared at the floor.
"Pandora," Fortisman said loudly. "Can you hear me?"
"Yes," the attendant mumbled.
"How long have you served Lady Catherine?"
"Three months." She was speaking more clearly now and Fortisman knew he didn't have much time before the drug wore off.

ÜBUNG 96 !

Übung 96: Lesen Sie weiter und formulieren Sie die Fragen aus der Perspektive von Lord Fortisman!

1. "Catherine go Edward's tower on the night of the feast?"

____?

"No," Pandora replied.

2. "anyone go there?"

____?

"Yes."

3. "you see who be?"

____?

"Yes. It was me."

4. "you know how Edward die?"

____?

"Yes. He was poisoned."

5. “where you get poison?”

____?

“It was given to me.”

“Good gracious,” Stoutham exclaimed. “She murdered Edward.”
Pandora gave her head a shake and her eyes started to become clearer. She blinked a few times.
“Who gave you the poison?” Fortisman asked.
“It…was…”, Pandora said shaking her head again, starting to come around, “…Baron Hoodwink. He said he would reward me generously once he had inherited Fortisman Castle.”
“Good gracious,” Stoutham said again. “How many skeletons are there in your closet, Lord Fortisman?”
Fortisman began to answer but the pastor spoke first.
“Baron Hoodwink’s still in the castle,” he said. “And Anne’s in danger.”
Fortisman stepped towards Pandora and hit her hard in the face. She fell to the floor.
“My lord, what have I done to offend you?” she asked, stunned by the blow. She was very much awake now.
White with anger, Lord Fortisman would have hit her again, but was stopped by the pastor, who said softly, “It’s Baron Hoodwink you want. She has been led into evil.”
“But, Pastor”, Fortisman protested, “she murdered Edward.”
“She isn’t responsible. Throw her in the dungeon but spare her life.”
Fortisman turned to Stoutham. “Lord Stoutham, what do you advise?”
“We must find Baron Hoodwink,” Stoutham said. “We can deal with this stupid servant girl later.”

Pandora began crying on the floor, knowing that the men knew her secrets.

"My lord", she pleaded, falling at the feet of Lord Fortisman, "I beg you. Spare my life."

Fortisman went to the door and called for some guards. Sir Stalwart came into the chamber with three men.

"We can't find Baron Hoodwink, my lord," Stalwart explained. "His horse isn't in the stable either. We believe he has left the castle."

"Aaargh!" Fortisman shouted again. "He must have escaped when he saw Pandora come into my chamber. Prepare our horses. We'll go after him at once."

Stoutham stood up from his chair, eager to be a part of the chase. In doing so, his robe got caught on one of the arms of the chair, causing it to open. Pandora saw the handle of a dagger sticking out of the top of Stoutham's right boot. The men were not watching her and she crawled along the floor and grabbed the dagger. Stoutham saw her and as she tried to hit Fortisman with the knife, he quickly moved in front and took the hit, the knife going deep into his leg. He shouted with pain and fell to the floor, blood already running onto the wood.

ÜBUNG 97

Übung 97: Welche Gegenteile gehören zusammen? Ordnen Sie zu!

1. deep	☐ lost
2. stand up	☐ shout
3. truth	☐ sit down
4. found	☐ shallow
5. whisper	☐ lie

"Lord Stoutham," Fortisman shouted.
"Fear not, it's just a scratch," Stoutham said, a thin smile on his face.
"Take this wicked witch away," Fortisman ordered.
The guards came forward and Pandora fought against them until they managed to restrain her.
"The magnificent Baron Hoodwink will get his revenge," she shouted. "And he will become King of England."
The guards started to drag Pandora from the chamber.
"Stop!" Fortisman ordered. He reached into the pocket of his robe and took out the potion his uncle had given him last night, the one that was supposed to make him courageous in battle. He narrowed his eyes at the bottle and then took off the top. He walked over to Pandora.
"Hold her mouth open."
The guards struggled but managed to get her mouth open and Fortisman forced her to swallow the potion. Her body shook a little and then became limp. She did not utter a sound. The pastor stopped attending Stoutham's wound and went to her.
"She's dead," he said and crossed himself. "May God have mercy on her soul."
The guards carried her from the room.
"He tried to give me poison," Fortisman shouted, throwing the bottle against the wall in anger.
Pastor Matthew went back to attending Stoutham's wound.
"It's not so bad," the pastor said. "Be strong, my lord. I'll now withdraw the dagger."
Stoutham gritted his teeth. "It's not my first wound, but the first from a woman."
He shouted with pain as the pastor took the knife out. The blade was shiny and red with noble blood.

A servant came in with some white cloth and the pastor quickly secured the wound. The bleeding stopped. Thirsty, Lord Stoutham reached out for his goblet of wine but took the wine with the truth potion inside by mistake.

"Oh dear," he said, realizing his mistake. His face went blank and his voice went flat. "Thank goodness my leg was so fat that the knife couldn't go in very far."

"Take him to one of the guests' chambers and lay him on the bed," Fortisman ordered. "And do not under any circumstances ask him any questions."

Stoutham was carried from the room. "Women are a dangerous breed," he cursed.

"Come, my lord," said Sir Stalwart. "Our horses will be waiting for us."

"There's not a moment to lose," Fortisman said as he dashed from his chamber.

The men ran outside the castle and mounted their horses. They galloped across the lowered drawbridge, but Stalwart ordered them to stop. They all looked down at the moat and saw the body of Anne floating on the surface.

"Oh my God! No!" Fortisman exclaimed.

ÜBUNG 98 !

Übung 98: Stimmen die Aussagen? Markieren Sie mit richtig ✔ oder falsch – !

1. Lord Stoutham killed Edward. ☐
2. Pandora is dead. ☐
3. Baron Hoodwink is Lord Fortisman's brother. ☐
4. Baron Hoodwink was at the engagement party. ☐
5. The feud between the Stouthams and Fortismans is over. ☐

Chapter 8: Revenge Is Taken

Fortisman was first to dismount his horse and ran to the moat. Rain began to fall in large drops, splashing the moat and making loud slapping sounds as the raindrops hit Fortisman's hat and coat. He bent down to the moat and managed to reach one of Anne's arms. He lifted her from the water and lay her on the grass. Her face was pale and she showed no signs of life.

"Someone get the pastor, immediately," Fortisman ordered. He stroked the pale cheeks of his daughter's face. He was surprised that her face was slightly warm. She coughed loudly and then spat out some of the moat's green water.

"Anne," Fortisman shouted. The men gasped in surprise, as if seeing someone come back from the dead. "Are you all right?"

Anne coughed again. She sat up. Fortisman took her in his arms.

"A man in black dragged me up to the tower", she explained, "and pushed me through the window."

"Hoodwink," Fortisman hissed.

"I didn't get a good look at him. I only saw that he was bald."

"Don't worry, Anne," Fortisman said. "We'll catch the villain." He turned to his guards. "Find Hoodwink's attendant and keep the drawbridge raised."

Some of the guards ran back into the castle. Then Pastor Matthew appeared with some servants.

"Oh no," the pastor exclaimed running towards Fortisman and Anne. "Is she all right?"

"She was pushed from the window by Hoodwink's attendant," Fortisman explained. "But she survived the fall."

"She's without doubt a Fortisman," the pastor said. "Both strong and lucky."

Fortisman nodded and then helped Anne to her feet.

"Take her to her room so she can rest and make sure the room is guarded," he said. Then he turned to his noblemen. "Mount your horses," he shouted. "We have a murderer to catch."
The men cheered and mounted their horses. They followed the tracks of one horse into the forest but the heavy rain soon made the tracks disappear. They reached the centre of the forest but were forced to stop.
"Aaargh!" Fortisman shouted. "The tracks have been washed away."
"My lord", said Sir Stalwart, "I suggest we split up."

ÜBUNG 99 !

Übung 99: Setzen Sie die Verben in Klammern in die richtige Zeitform!

Lord Fortisman (1. stroke) _______________ his beard. He (2. look) _______________ into the trees and couldn't help (3. feel) _______________ he was being (4. watch) _______________. There were groups of outlaws who (5. move) _______________ into the forest (6. hide) _______________ from the law.

"Yes, Sir Stalwart," Fortisman said. "You stay with me. The rest of you, split into groups of three and search the forest. Baron Hoodwink can't be far. And as long as I am alive, his work is left unfinished. We'll meet back at the castle in one hour. But nobody is allowed to kill him. That pleasure will be mine."
The men formed themselves into small groups and rode off in different directions. They soon disappeared amongst the trees and Fortisman was alone with Sir Stalwart.

“My lord?” the nobleman asked as he watched Fortisman looking into the trees thoughtfully.
“Follow me, Sir Stalwart. I think I know where he is.”
Fortisman kicked his horse and Stalwart followed close behind. They rode along a narrow path in silence until they came to the base of a small and rocky mountain.
“Look,” Sir Stalwart said, his eyes still sharp even though he was aging. “There’s a horse tethered in the trees.”
Fortisman nodded and then looked up at the smoke coming from the cave about half way up the mountain.
“He’s here.”
They tied their horses further in the forest and then walked back to the mountain.
“What is this place?” Stalwart asked.
“Keep your wits about you, Sir Stalwart,” Fortisman whispered. “A powerful sorcerer lives in a cave on this mountain.”
“A maker of potions?”
Fortisman nodded. “I believe he supplied Baron Hoodwink with the poison that killed Edward, and another poison meant for me.”
Stalwart pulled out his long sword. Fortisman did the same and the two men walked up the narrow mountain path with swords in their hands.
“Wait here, my lord,” Sir Stalwart whispered at the entrance to the cave. “I can’t put you in danger.”
“No,” Fortisman said pulling the nobleman back. “Concocto doesn’t like strangers. And if Baron Hoodwink’s here, then the sorcerer may have magic prepared, powerful magic that our swords will be useless against.”
“There’s nothing more powerful than a sword in the hands of a nobleman,” Sir Stalwart said, insulted. He didn’t believe in magic and sorcery; he thought it was all nonsense.

"Let me go in first," Fortisman said. "But follow close behind me. They may be surprised to see us, so don't make any sudden moves, and beware of the mysterious sorcerer."
They edged toward the entrance of the cave. There was a lot of smoke as always and Fortisman couldn't see past it. It was like walking with his eyes closed, or like walking through the fog of some childhood nightmare.
"I have a bad feeling about this, my lord," Sir Stalwart whispered.
The two men edged into the main room of the cave. The smoke was coming from a large cauldron on a fire and the sorcerer was hunched over it, stirring with a large spoon. Fortisman wondered briefly if the sorcerer did anything else other than stand over his cauldron.
"Welcome, my lord," Concocto said. "I thought you might come. The potion I gave you seldom fails. Do you need more?"
"I'm not here for potions," Fortisman said looking around the room. It was quite dark and he saw numerous places where a man could hide himself. He felt sick with fear and would have felt braver facing an army on a battlefield than cornered in the sorcerer's dark cave.
"Then why are you here?" asked Concocto. "And with such a burly and aggressive nobleman? I must say, his sword is most impressive. Is he compensating for his God-given weapons of lesser size?"
Stalwart grunted loudly and tried to move past Fortisman, but the lord held him back.
"We're looking for a villain," Fortisman said, his eyes moving around the room. "A customer of yours."
"I have many customers", the sorcerer replied, "and many of them are villains, even those who pretend to be otherwise."
"This villain is dressed in black."
The sorcerer smiled, showing his stained and crooked teeth. "Well,

villains seem to prefer to colour of night and shadows, so they can hide more easily."

"He bought the poison from you that killed Edward," Fortisman said.

"Poison is poison, but what men do with it I cannot be blamed for."

Sir Stalwart moved forward. "You evil wizard," he shouted, his anger making him lose control. "You're responsible for Edward's murder."

He slipped past Fortisman and rushed at the sorcerer with his sword raised in the air.

"Sir Stalwart, no!" Fortisman shouted. He reached out to stop the nobleman but was too slow.

Stalwart was about to land a blow on the sorcerer but Concocto was quicker and moved aside. The sword swung through the air and hit the metal of the cauldron with a loud clang. With Stalwart off-balance, the sorcerer reached into his pocket and threw a red powder into Stalwart's eyes. He dropped his sword and stumbled backwards towards the cave wall, rubbing his eyes and screaming with pain. Then his screaming stopped as the silver streak of a sword came through his stomach. It was quickly withdrawn again and Stalwart fell to the ground.

"I'm responsible for Edward's murder," Baron Hoodwink said as he emerged from the shadows, Stalwart's blood dripping from the tip of his sword. "And I'll do the same to you and take back what's rightfully mine."

Fortisman held out his sword. As Hoodwink moved closer, Fortisman was again surprised to see what an old man his uncle was, with a heavily lined and scarred face and small black eyes that seemed forever narrowed.

"Noblemen", the sorcerer began, "I do not wish my cave to become a battleground. Lower your swords."

"Stay out of this, sorcerer," Hoodwink ordered. "I want this to be a personal victory."
"The victory will be mine", Fortisman replied, raising his sword, "and I don't need your so-called bravery potion."

Übung 100: Unterstreichen Sie die zwölf Substantive des folgenden Textabschnitts!

The sorcerer stepped back. He took a bottle from his shelf of potions and went over to the body of Sir Stalwart. With what looked like water, he washed the red powder from the nobleman's eyes and face. Sir Stalwart groaned loudly and put two hands over his stomach.

Fortisman and Hoodwink faced each other, the tips of their swords almost touching. They shuffled slowly around in a circle, each waiting for the other to move first.
"Pandora's dead and Anne's alive," Fortisman said. "She survived the fall."
"Accursed misfortune!" Hoodwink shouted. "My servant should have used a knife. I'll kill her after I finish you off."
He lifted his sword to strike but Fortisman warded off the blow. Their swords scratched and clanged each time they were struck together, almost sending off sparks. Fortisman was surprised by the old man's strength and found himself on the defensive, moving backwards around the cave and fending off numerous strikes. Hoodwink saw his advantage and became more aggressive, swinging his heavy sword around like it was but a feather, trying to land one fatal blow.
"I am the rightful heir of Fortisman Castle," he shouted. He raised

his sword high and swung it down sideways to cut off Fortisman's head. The lord ducked just in time, but the sword cut his shoulder and he yelled with pain. He dashed backwards to recover himself. The baron laughed arrogantly, knowing victory would be his.

"Your father was also poor with the sword," he said. "More suited to matters of the court than to battle just like you. When I become Lord of Fortisman Castle, the whole of England will shake with fear at the mere mention of my name."

Fortisman grimaced and took his sword in both hands. His shoulder burned with pain and blood trickled down his right arm and onto the handle of the sword making it sticky and difficult to grip. He moved forward, his anger giving him strength. He swung his sword powerfully and forced Hoodwink onto the defensive. Fortisman edged Hoodwink towards the wall where Concocto was still attending to the wound of Sir Stalwart. Fortisman briefly caught the nobleman's eyes and was surprised to see life in them. Stalwart smiled and managed to extend one of his legs. Hoodwink tripped over the leg and stumbled just enough to lose his balance. Fortisman moved forward and drove his sword right into his uncle's heart.

"Aaargh!" Hoodwink screamed as he fell to the floor, the sword sticking out of his chest.

Fortisman stood over him and placed one boot on his uncle's chest.

"Murderer," he hissed. And then he pulled the sword from Hoodwink's chest causing him to again scream with pain, as if his heart had been pulled from his chest as well.

"Please," he said, his words coming with difficulty. Blood trickled out of his mouth and dripped from his chin. "I'm dying. You've won, but bury me in Fortisman Castle. Lay me next to my brother where I belong."

"I'll do no such thing," Fortisman said angrily.

Stunned that his last request was denied, the baron shouted with his last breath, "You'll never be King of England."

ÜBUNG 101

Übung 101: Finden Sie ein Synonym zu den Wörtern in Klammern!

Then his head (1. go down) __________ back against the earth floor and his chest (2. cease) __________ moving up and down. Fortisman (3. to move) __________ over to Sir Stalwart and (4. go lower) __________ down to look at the nobleman's (5. injury) __________. There was blood everywhere and Fortisman knew the blow would be (6. deadly) __________.

"Well fought, my lord," Stalwart whispered, his voice breathless.
"It's just a scratch, isn't it?" Fortisman asked.
"I think not. But I'll die knowing that I served a great and powerful lord."
"Do something, Concocto," Fortisman ordered.
The sorcerer shrugged. "Causing death is easy, but stopping it is beyond my power."
"My lord", Stalwart said, his eyes almost closed, "take me back to the castle and lay me in your tomb."
"Stay strong, Sir Stalwart," Fortisman said. "I'll get you back to the castle and the pastor will save you."
The nobleman managed a weak smile. "No. I'm gone. I survived so many battles and end up dying with a sword through my back in the cave of a sorcerer."
"The powder was only meant to blind you for a few moments,"

Concocto said lightly. "I warned Lord Fortisman never to attack a sorcerer. I had no intention of killing you."

Stalwart snarled at the sorcerer. "You do the work of the devil," he said, and then he coughed loudly and spat out blood.

"I do only work," Concocto replied. "I'm a man of science."

Stalwart coughed again and the pain made him close his eyes. He turned to Fortisman.

"Live long, my lord", he said softly, "and know that you'll make a great king."

Fortisman nodded and then watched as the life left Sir Stalwart's eyes.

"My cave has never seen so much killing," Concocto said. "It's normally a place of work and experiment."

"But this was all your doing," Fortisman said angrily. "I have half a mind to take you down with my sword."

The sorcerer looked at Fortisman, his one eye blazing. "You cannot blame me for the evil acts that men do. If you do, then I can also blame your sword maker for making the sword that killed Baron Hoodwink."

Fortisman frowned. He did not want to admit it, but the sorcerer was right.

"When I'm King of England," he declared. "I want you to become a member of my court. I could use your services. The courts are full of enemies and spies and a man of science and magic would come in very handy."

"That's a very generous offer, my lord, but I'm afraid Baron Hoodwink was right. You will not become king."

Fortisman was stunned. "But how can you know this?"

"The next line of kings will come from the highlands," the sorcerer said. He walked back to his cauldron and stirred the contents. "I have foreseen it."

"From the highlands?" Fortisman exclaimed. "That's impossible. England will never be ruled by a Scot."

"It may seem strange", the sorcerer conceded, "but it will be so. You shall not be the one who succeeds Queen Elizabeth."

Fortisman frowned at the sorcerer and then walked over to the body of Sir Stalwart and lifted him up. He grunted as the pain throbbed in his wounded shoulder.

"I'll come back for Baron Hoodwink."

Lord Fortisman carried Stalwart out of the cave, down the mountain and then secured him to his horse. He rode alone through the forest and back to Fortisman Castle. Hoodwink's attendant had been captured but Fortisman took little pleasure in cutting off the man's bald head.

He had got his revenge but he seemed only to feel worse for it. His wife had been right. All the killing had not brought Edward back and had not eased his pain. He retired to his chamber, went to the bookshelf for the container of grey powder and tried to remember that happy tune Edward had once played on the cembalo.

ÜBUNG 102 !

Übung 102: Beantworten Sie die Fragen zum Text!

1. Who went up to Edward's tower on the night of the murder?

____

2. Who pushed Anne out of the window?

____

3. How did Concocto prevent Sir Stalwart from stabbing him?

____

4. Who will become the next king of England according to the sorcerer?

---

5. Where will Sir Stalwart be buried?

After the due period of mourning had passed, a feast celebrating the new alliance between the two families was held at Stoutham Castle because Lord Stoutham's wounded leg meant he was still unable to travel. He and Lord Fortisman sat at the long table, their wives at their sides, and laughed like old friends. Everyone was merry and enjoying themselves.

"By the way", Stoutham said leaning close to Fortisman, "have you heard the news from London? Her Majesty is in excellent health. They say she's as feisty as ever and could live another ten years."

"That's excellent news," Fortisman said forcing a smile. "But enough talk of politics. I have a surprise."

On his signal the music stopped and a stage was quickly prepared in front of the long table.

"Oh, a play," exclaimed Lord Stoutham. "How did you know I was so keen on the theatre?"

"This is a very special play." Fortisman said to his wife and was surprised to see a single tear run down her cheek. But she smiled because she was proud of her husband for organizing the performance and also happy that the old feud had finally come to an end.

An actor walked onto the stage and declared loudly, "Welcome lords, ladies and noblemen, to the first ever performance of 'The Noble Playwright', a play in three acts by Edward Fortisman."

THE END

Abschlusstest

Übung 1: Welches Wort ist das „schwarze Schaf"?

1. brew, potion, water, drug
2. murderer, victim, killer, criminal
3. mountain, river, forest, castle
4. destroy, make, produce, construct
5. fear, worry, panic, courage

Übung 2: Formulieren Sie die Sätze als Frage!

1. Lord Fortisman know who killer be

____?

2. be the best way Stoutham Castle

____?

3. can Concocto know who next king be

____?

4. where Lady Fortisman get beautiful dress

____?

5. give Edward poison

____?

6. wrote the play staged at Stoutham Castle

____?

Übung 3: Ordnen Sie die die Sätze zu einer sinnvollen Dialogsequenz!

1. "Yes, servant, what is it?"
2. "That's terrible news. Did she say why?"
3. "And?"
4. "Thank you, servant. You may go."
5. "Enter."
6. "She has to travel to Scotland for an important meeting."
7. "She sends her regards but cannot attend the funeral."
8. "Good morning, my lord."
9. "I bring you news from the Queen."

Lösung: _ _ _ _ _ _ _ _ _ _

Übung 4: Formulieren Sie if-Sätze!

1. The Queen comes. It be a great honour.

___

2. I knew the answer. I tell you.

___

3. He had taken the truth potion. He tell the truth.

___

4. I was King. I not allow this.

___

5. Edward had not died. He inherit Fortisman Castle.

____

6. He insults me. I kill him.

____

Übung 5: Setzen Sie die richtigen Präpositionen ein!

The castle is located (1.) ______ a forest. It has a moat (2.) ______ it and two high towers (3.) ______ either side. Lord Fortisman is the owner (4.) ______ the castle and lives there (5.) ______ his wife. He has lived (6.) ______ the castle his entire life. There is a picture (7.) ______ him (8.) ______ the wall (9.) ______ the main hall.

Übung 6: Welche Gegenteile gehören zusammen? Ordnen Sie zu!

1. guilty	☐ narrow
2. courageous	☐ deny
3. respect	☐ contempt
4. murderer	☐ shallow
5. accuse	☐ victim
6. dawn	☐ weak
7. wide	☐ cowardly
8. strong	☐ dusk
9. deep	☐ innocent

Übung 7: Formulieren Sie die Sätze im Passiv!

1. Somebody has murdered Edward.

____

2. We will find the killer.

____

3. Leave Catherine alone.

____

4. We were drinking wine when thc murder happened.

____

5. I am not going to forgive him.

____

Übung 8: Setzen Sie die Verben in die richtige Zeitform!

He (1. approach) ______________ the castle at a gallop. The watchman (2. see) ______________ him just in time and the draw-bridge was (3. lower) ______________ quickly enough so that Fortisman (4. do not) ______________ have to (5. slow down) ______________ his horse. He (6. ride) ______________ into the castle courtyard where several servants (7. rush) ______________ out to meet him.

Übung 9: Übersetzen Sie und enträtseln Sie das Lösungswort!

1. Wahrheit _ □ _ _ _
2. Mut _ _ _ _ _ _ □
3. Schurke □ _ _ _ _ _ _
4. Erbe _ □ _ _
5. Trank _ _ _ _ _ □
6. schuldig □ _ _ _ _ _
7. Vergebung _ _ _ _ _ _ □ _ _ _ _

Lösung: _ _ _ _ _ _ _

Übung 10: Beantworten Sie die Fragen zum Text!

1. Who killed Edward?

____

2. What is the relationship between Baron Hoodwink and Lord Fortisman?

____

3. Who killed Sir Stalwart?

____

4. Why is there a feast held at Stoutham Castle?

____

Lösungen

Übung 1: 1. The powerful sorcerer lives in a cave. 2. The man took his sword in his right hand. 3. One eye was covered by a patch. 4. The man's hat and coat were out of fashion. 5. The smoke came from a large cauldron.

Übung 2: 1. amount 2. smoke 3. bottle 4. small 5. voice 6. mouth 7. coat 8. money Lösung: nobleman

Übung 3: 1. b 2. a 3. b 4. b 5. a

Übung 4: 1. office 2. dog 3. mother 4. gun 5. Thursday 6. ride 7. mountain

Übung 5: 1. dragged 2. move 3. was 4. had worked 5. stumbled 6. thumping 7. stopped 8. pointed 9. floating

Übung 6: 1. castle 2. moat 3. stable-boy 4. drawbridge 5. sword 6. forest 7. queen

Übung 7: 1. people 2. around 3. anyone 4. forward 5. knocked 6. disturb 7. morning

Übung 8: 1. When did you find my son? 2. We must tell Lord Fortisman the news. 3. We will depart in ten minutes. 4. The man in black smiled in the darkness. 5. Lady Fortisman fell to her knees and cried.

Übung 9: 1. to 2. inside 3. on 4. over 5. by 6. to 7. In 8. of

Übung 10: 1. better 2. more interested 3. longer 4. younger 5. older 6. earlier

Übung 11: 1. slowly 2. loudly 3. quickly 4. sadly 5. angrily 6. hard 7. thinly

Übung 12: 1. light/dark 2. alive/dead 3. dawn/dusk 4. asleep/awake 5. loud/quiet 6. short/long

Übung 13: 1. right 2. many 3. cheered 4. hungry 5. angered 6. murdered

Übung 14: 1. Edward is dead. 2. The body was found in the castle moat. 3. The stable-boy found the body. 4. Lord Fortisman thinks Lord Stoutham is the killer. 5. They are brother and sister.

Übung 15: 1. audience 2. rival 3. response 4. support 5. reaction 6. battle 7. religious

Übung 16: 1. a 2. b 3. a

Übung 17: 1. The announcement of the wedding between Edward and Catherine was celebrated last night. 2. No, they are going to be married. 3. No, Lord Fortisman checked whether Catherine was in her chamber. 4. Anne is Edward's sister, she is at the royal court in London. 5. Lady Fortisman convinces Lord Fortisman to ride to Stoutham Castle unarmed.

Übung 18: brisk, pale, last, wet, fresh, cold, earlier, young

Übung 19: 1. The horse was kicked by Lord Fortisman. 2. Their arrival was not announced. 3. The horses were slowed to a trot. 4. The food is being eaten and the wine is being drunk by the guests. 5. He was snapped from his musings by the cold air.

Übung 20: 1. look (looked) 2. rust (rusted) 3. up (down) 4. saw (see) 5. float (floating) 6. surprising (surprised) 7. any (some) 8. grass (water)

Übung 21: 1. for 2. to 3. for 4. through 5. to 6. at 7. of 8. to 9. for
Übung 22: 1. I would like an audience with Lord Stoutham. 2. Tie your horses to the tree. 3. We come without weapons. 4. The attendant spoke with someone else. 5. Stoutham Castle's colours are blue and red.
Übung 23: 1. guarded 2. widening 3. was 4. have seen 5. had left 6. celebrating 7. was 8. did
Übung 24: 1. smile/frown 2. strength/weakness 3. stay/leave 4. raise/lower 5. the same/different 6. cowardly/brave 7. in front of/behind 8. familiar/strange
Übung 25: 1. is speaking 2. rode 3. is/was looking 4. was 5. has lived
Übung 26: 1. weapons 2. recognize 3. preparation 4. garments 5. search 6. outdated
Übung 27: 1. Edward/Lord Fortisman's son 2. Concocto/sorcerer 3. Sir Stalwart/nobleman 4. William/Lord Fortisman's young brother 5. Elizabeth I/Queen of England 6. Matthew/pastor 7. Lady Fortisman/sister of Lord Stoutham
Übung 28: 1. it's 2. he's 3. didn't 4. he's 5. I've 6. didn't
Übung 29: 1. smell 2. early 3. attendant 4. sportsman 5. boots 6. shy 7. happy 8. wide
Übung 30: brightly, still, forever, intently, seriously, intensely, really, hard, thoughtfully, absolutely
Übung 31: 1. falsch 2. richtig 3. falsch 4. falsch 5. richtig 6. richtig 7. falsch
Übung 32: 1. voice 2. murderer 3. terrible 4. shocked 5. lifeless 6. window
Übung 33: 1. Someone saw the murderer riding towards Stoutham Castle. 2. The news shocked Lord Stoutham. 3. They are putting the peace to the test. 4. No one will speak to Lord Fortisman like that. 5. They didn't recognize any of the guards.
Übung 34: 1. What 2. How 3. Where 4. When 5. Why 6. Who
Übung 35: 1. quickly 2. ran 3. tell 4. go back 5. attack 6. mounted 7. collect 8. assemble
Übung 36: 1. valuable 2. heir 3. royal 4. insult 5. attack 6. mistrust 7. crown Lösung: villain
Übung 37: 1. noisy 2. cowardly 3. deserted 4. dishonest 5. thin
Übung 38: morning's, events, eyes, watch, night, castle, night, head, music, singing, night, watch
Übung 39: 1. When did he fall asleep? 2. Where did you find the wine jug? 3. What colour did Donald's face turn? 4. Why did he fall asleep? 5. Why didn't he see the murderer?
Übung 40: 1. you 2. You 3. She 4. it 5. it 6. he 7. He 8. it
Übung 41: 1. This conversation is amusing. 2. Who brought you the wine? 3. Give me one reason why I should not cut off your head. 4. I think that Edward was pushed from the tower. 5. The music kept me from falling asleep.
Übung 42: 1. throwing (threw) 2. angry (angrily) 3. from (out of) 4. feet (hands) 5. luked (looked) 6. surpraise (surprise) 7. storm (stormed) 8. clutched (clutching)

Übung 43: 1. b 2. b 3. a
Übung 44: 1. smiled 2. stroked 3. fell 4. thrown 5. have seen 6. have survived 7. is
Übung 45: 1. Lord Fortisman might become King of England. 2. The pastor always advises Fortisman very well. 3. Lord Stoutham was insulted by the accusation. 4. Donald is sitting in the dungeon. 5. Sir Stalwart always tries to defend his men.
Übung 46: 1. sensitive 2. politician 3. killer 4. attack 5. convinced 6. window 7. peace
Übung 47: Would you please put him in the dungeon. 2. I would like you to find him, please. 3. Would you mind leaving my castle, please. 4. I would ask you not to talk to Lord Fortisman in that way, please. 5. I would like some wine, please. 6. Would you please leave me alone, Pastor Matthew.
Übung 48: 1. rubbed 2. looked 3. had played 4. was 5. had watched 6. had fought 7. had been 8. had become
Übung 49: 1. It is located in the east wing of the castle. 2. There is a cembalo in the chamber. 3. Donald was thrown in the dungeon. 4. He fell asleep on his watch and didn't see Edward's murderer. 5. The pastor has green eyes. 6. Donald is sent to Stoutham Castle as a spy.
Übung 50: 1. strongly 2. carefully 3. thinly 4. definitely 5. hopefully 6. terribly 7. softly 8. defensively
Übung 51: 1. to 2. to 3. during 4. in 5. in 6. by 7. to 8. off
Übung 52: 1. kaltblütig 2. Waffenstillstand 3. Reitkunst 4. unbegründet 5. Spionage 6. Waffen
Übung 53: 1. richtig 2. falsch 3. falsch 4. richtig 5. falsch 6. falsch
Übung 54: 1. entered 2. greet 3. wore 4. pretty 5. began 6. leave 7. forgive
Übung 55: 1. b 2. a 3. a
Übung 56: 1. powder 2. liquid 3. transparent 4. staggered 5. remember 6. notes 7. cembalo 8. fingers
Übung 57: 1. stare at 2. accuse 3. curtsy 4. suspect 5. grimace 6. smooth
Übung 58: lord, nobleman, mistake, night, dungeon, chains, time, lord, teeth, actions, guards, weapons, murderer, castle, plot
Übung 59: 1. b 2. c 3. a
Übung 60: 1. to 2. of 3. to 4. upon 5. to 6. in 7. across 8. into
Übung 61: 1. lives 2. rode 3. could have become 4. jumped 5. had been 6. was waiting
Übung 62: looked, are, smiled, felt, did, pass, make, reach, was murdered, admitted, has been
Übung 63: 1. full/empty 2. safe/dangerous 3. narrow/wide 4. thin/thick 5. heavy/light 6. exit/entrance 7. large/small
Übung 64: 1. A bottle was given to Fortisman by Concocto. 2. Secrets are carried by men their whole lives. 3. A measure of potion is being poured into a bot-

tle by Concocto. 4. The bottle was turned upside down by him. 5. A pouch of coins was dropped on the table by Lord Fortisman.

Übung 65: 1. rode 2. had not told 3. had not denied 4. knew 5. were 6. meant 7. murdered 8. thought

Übung 66: 1. falsch 2. richtig 3. falsch 4. richtig 5. falsch 6. richtig

Übung 67: 1. Who 2. What 3. Where 4. How 5. When 6. Why

Übung 68: 1. stare 2. furniture 3. together 4. sheets 5. snakes 6. eager 7. shock 8. letter

Übung 69: 1. He said he had an important errand to run. 2. He said he would visit her in her chamber. 3. He said the messenger was riding to London. 4. He said you were not fit to travel. 5. He said he had not seen him today. 6. He said delivering news to the Queen could sometimes be difficult.

Übung 70: 1. peaceful 2. arguing 3. smiled 4. intention 5. continued 6. come 7. pretending

Übung 71: 1. queen 2. argument 3. mirror 4. clever 5. silk Lösung: quill

Übung 72: 1. throwed (threw) 2. standing (stood) 3. weared (wore) 4. is (was) 5. was having (had) 6. had been turning (turned)

Übung 73: 1. No, Lord Stoutham didn't buy any weapons from Donald. 2. Lord Fortisman stopped at the inn. 3. Concocto has only one eye because he used one of his eyes for a potion. 4. Lady Fortisman is writing a letter to her daughter Anne. 5. Lord Fortisman suggests to his wife that she should go to bed and sleep away her mad thoughts.

Übung 74: 1. metal 2. worthless 3. cloudy 4. king 5. friend 6. solid

Übung 75: 1. at 2. to 3. at 4. of 5. of 6. in 7. of 8. to 9. in

Übung 76: 1. The queen sends her warmest regards. 2. He read the letter until he fell asleep. 3. She wrote the letter with a quill. 4. He almost dropped the bottle of potion. 5. The messenger handed the letter to Lord Fortisman.

Übung 77: 1. laughter 2. geniuses 3. forever 4. mocking 5. heart 6. sarcastically 7. words

Übung 78: Lösung: 4, 5, 1, 7, 2, 6, 3

Übung 79: 1. a 2. b 3. b

Übung 80: 1. locked 2. creaking 3. saw 4. scattered 5. saw 6. had argued 7. wanting 8. went 9. was covered

Übung 81: 1. I can't believe he wrote a play. 2. Edward wanted to go to London. 3. Fortisman hasn't found the killer yet. 4. I was going to tell you but I forgot. 5. I will never allow you to leave the castle.

Übung 82: 1. popular/unknown 2. interesting/dull 3. allow/forbid 4. respect/contempt 5. sorrow/joy 6. nobleman/commoner 7. clean/stained 8. shame/pride

Übung 83: 1. a 2. c 3. b

Übung 84: 1. wonders (wondering) 2. going (gone) 3. became (become) 4. suxessful (successful) 5. being (been) 6. kaused (caused) 7. sertainly (certainly) 8. is (was) 9. sun (son)

Übung 85: 1. No, she won't attend Edward's funeral. 2. Edward wanted to be a writer. 3. Edward admired Shakespeare, Marlowe and Jonson. 4. Catherine comes to Edward's chamber. 5. They had planned to go to London.
Übung 86: 1. funeral 2. church 3. altar 4. robe 5. garments 6. artist 7. nobleman
Übung 87: 1. "Lord Fortisman is sad." 2. "I fear dark forces are at work." 3. "I cannot think of anything else." 4. "I will find the killer." 5. "I'm going to leave next week."
Übung 88: 1. falsch 2. richtig 3. falsch 4. falsch 5. richtig 6. falsch
Übung 89: corners, eyes, direction, attention, guests, castle gatherings, celebrations, people, guests, engagement party
Übung 90: 1. Who 2. When 3. How 4. Where 5. What 6. Why
Übung 91: 1. to 2. with 3. to 4. of 5. into 6. up 7. to 8. in
Übung 92: 1. alcoholic 2. theoretical 3. honourable 4. extremely 5. well 6. good
Übung 93: 1. dishonourable 2. struggled 3. arms 4. understand 5. death 6. anger 7. acted
Übung 94: 1. If Fortisman finds the killer, he will kill him. 2. If Edward was still alive, he would go to London. 3. If Donald had been awake, he would have seen the murderer. 4. If you see her, say hello for me.
Übung 95: 1. likeable 2. sensitive 3. sort 4. valid 5. childlike
Übung 96: 1. "Did Catherine go to Edward's tower on the night of the feast?" 2. "Did anyone go there?" 3. "Did you see who it was?" 4. "Do you know how Edward died?" 5. "Where did you get the poison?"
Übung 97: 1. deep/shallow 2. stand up/sit down 3. truth/lie 4. found/lost 5. whisper/shout
Übung 98: 1. falsch 2. richtig 3. falsch 4. falsch 5. richtig
Übung 99: 1. stroked 2. looked 3. feeling 4. watched 5. had moved 6. hiding
Übung 100: sorcerer, bottle, shelf, potions, body, water, powder, nobleman's, eyes, face, hands, stomach
Übung 101: 1. fell 2. stopped 3. went 4. bent 5. wound 6. fatal
Übung 102: 1. Catherine's attendant Pandora went up to Edward's tower. 2. Baron Hoodwink's attendant pushed Anne out of the window. 3. Concocto threw a red powder into his face. 4. According to Concocto the next king of England will be a Scotsman. 5. Sir Stalwart will be buried at Fortisman castle.

Lösungen Abschlusstest

Übung 1: 1. water 2. victim 3. castle 4. destroy 5. courage
Übung 2: 1. Does Lord Fortisman know who the killer is? 2. What is the best way to Stoutham Castle? 3. How can Concocto know who the next king will be? 4. Where did Lady Fortisman get that beautiful dress? 5. Who gave Edward the poison? Who wrote the play staged at Stoutham Castle?
Übung 3: Lösung: 5, 8, 1, 9, 3, 7, 2, 6, 4
Übung 4: 1. If the Queen comes, it will be a great honour. 2. If I knew the answer, I would tell you. 3. If he had taken the truth potion, he would have told the truth. 4. If I was King, I would not allow this. 5. If Edward had not died, he would have inherited Fortisman Castle. 6. If he insults me, I will kill him.
Übung 5: 1. near 2. around 3. on 4. of 5. with 6. in 7. of 8. on 9. in
Übung 6: 1. guilty/innocent 2. courageous/cowardly 3. respect/contempt 4. murderer/victim 5. accuse/deny 6. dawn/dusk 7. wide/narrow 8. strong/weak 9. deep/shallow
Übung 7: 1. Edward has been murdered. 2. The killer will be found by us. 3. Catherine should/is to be left alone. 4. Wine was being drunk when the murder happened. 5. He is not going to be forgiven by me.
Übung 8: 1. approached 2. saw 3. lowered 4. did not 5. slow down 6. rode 7. rushed
Übung 9: 1. truth 2. courage 3. villain 4. heir 5. potion 6. guilty 7. forgiveness Lösung: revenge
Übung 10: 1. Catherine's attendant Pandora killed Edward. 2. They are uncle and nephew. 3. Baron Hoodwink killed Sir Stalwart. 4. The feast celebrates the new alliance between the two families.